Capilano College Library

WORLDWATCH REPORT 175

Powering China's Development

The Role of Renewable Energy

WITHDRAWN

RECEIVED DEC 1 7 2007 LIBRARY CAPILANO COLLEGE

D0746542

ERIC MARTINOT AND LI JUNFENG

LISA MASTNY, *EDITOR*

WORLDWATCH INSTITUTE, WASHINGTON, DC

·62299951
70110113

© Worldwatch Institute, November 2007
ISBN 13: 978-1-878071-83-5
ISBN 10: 1-878071-83-1
Library of Congress Control Number: 2007939629

Printed on paper that is 50 percent recycled, 30 percent
post-consumer waste, process chlorine free.

The views expressed are those of the authors and do not necessarily
represent those of the Worldwatch Institute; of its directors, officers, or staff;
or of its funding organizations.

On the cover: Dawn at Nan'ao Wind Farm in Guangdong province.
Photograph © Greenpeace/Xuan Canxiong. Photo courtesy of Li Junfeng

WITHDRAWN

Reprint and copyright information for one-time academic use of this material is available
by contacting Customer Service, Copyright Clearance Center, at +1 978-750-8400 (phone) or
+1 978-750-4744 (fax), or by writing to CCC, 222 Rosewood Drive, Danvers, MA 01923, USA.

Nonacademic and commercial users should contact the Worldwatch Institute's Business
Development Department by fax at +1 202-296-7365 or by email at wwpub@worldwatch.org.

Table of Contents

Figures, Tables, and Sidebars

Acknowledgments

This report benefited greatly from the contributions of the following co-authors and researchers: Yingling Liu, Janet Sawin, and Christopher Flavin (Worldwatch Institute); Ma Lingjuan (Chinese Renewable Energy Industries Association); Wang Zhongying and Gao Hu (Energy Research Institute); and Cathy Kunkel (Tsinghua University). Substantive contributions were also provided by Frank Haugwitz, Sebastian Meyer, and Zhang Xiliang. At Worldwatch, thanks go to Senior Editor Lisa Mastny, Communications Director Darcey Rakestraw, Director of Publications and Marketing Patricia Shyne, Communications Associate Julia Tier, and Stanford MAP Fellow James Russell for their efforts in production and outreach. The report was designed by Worldwatch Art Director Lyle Rosbotham, and Elisabeth Sipkes with Nuance Design Studio did the layout. A special thanks to the Blue Moon Fund and to the Tsinghua-BP Clean Energy Research and Education Center at Tsinghua University for their support.

About the Authors

Eric Martinot is a visiting professor at Tsinghua University in Beijing and a senior research fellow with the Worldwatch Institute. Prior to coming to China, he spent four years with the Global Environment Facility (GEF) at the World Bank, where he managed the renewable energy program for developing countries, guided strategy, and synthesized knowledge and experience with renewable energy markets, policies, and projects around the world. Prior to the GEF, he served as consultant to the United Nations, World Bank, and International Energy Agency. He also served as senior scientist with the Stockholm Environment Institute in Boston, as convening lead author for the Intergovernmental Panel on Climate Change (IPCC), and as adjunct professor at the University of Maryland and Tufts University. He is the author of over 65 publications, including the recent REN21/Worldwatch Institute *Renewables Global Status Report*. Eric holds a PhD and M.A. in Energy and Resources from the University of California at Berkeley and a B.S. in Electrical Engineering from the Massachusetts Institute of Technology. For more information, visit www.martinot.info.

Li Junfeng is Vice Chair of China's Renewable Energy Society and Deputy Director General of the Energy Research Institute (ERI) of the National Development and Reform Commission in Beijing, China. He also serves as Chair of ERI's Academic Committee, General Secretary of the Chinese Renewable Energy Industries Association, Vice-Chairman of both the Global Wind Energy Council and the REN21 Renewable Energy Policy Network, and Director of the Renewable Energy and Energy Efficiency Partnership in East Asia. During China's 10th Five-Year Plan (2001–05), Mr. Li facilitated implementation of a national technology development program for wind and solar and chaired the government's Sustainable Energy Task Force. He was also the lead author for China's 2005 Renewable Energy Law. Mr. Li has worked on renewable energy project development with the World Bank, Global Environment Facility, and United Nations Development Programme. He works on Clean Development Mechanism (CDM) and carbon trading issues and recently led development of the first CDM project in China. He has authored and contributed to many publications on renewable energy and carbon trading. For more information, visit www.eri.org.cn and www.creia.net.

Preface

Increasingly, people around the world are becoming aware of China's rapidly growing energy needs and of the unprecedented levels of coal combustion needed to satiate this appetite. The results of this coal dependence are clear: China's citizens are suffering from some of the worst pollution in history, while the nation's carbon dioxide emissions are adding to the significant climate burden already imposed by the emissions of industrial countries.

When I visited Beijing in April 2007, I was struck as before by the dense layer of smog that obscures the impressive mountain ranges north of the city. But during my week of meetings in the Chinese capital, I was even more impressed by another story that is beginning to unfold: the near-explosive growth of the wind and solar energy industries. China's production of wind turbines and solar cells both more than doubled in 2006. The country is on track to rival the world's leaders in wind power and solar photovoltaics—in Europe, Japan, and North America—and it already dominates the markets for solar hot water and small hydropower.

As our two Beijing-based authors explain, China's meteoric rise in the most dynamic of today's energy sectors can be traced to a combination of policy leadership and entrepreneurial acumen. The country's new Renewable Energy Law, adopted by the National Peoples' Congress in February 2005, is the product of an extensive process of international research and consultation, as planners within the powerful National Development and Reform Commission sought to learn from the successes and failures of other nations.

We at Worldwatch are pleased to have played a small role in advising the Chinese government on that policy and are impressed by the strength and potential of the law that emerged. No less impressive in our view is the rapid growth of China's renewables industry. This is particularly true in solar energy, where a dozen start-up companies have entered the business in the past few years, many of them fueled with venture capital from international investors.

Renewable energy will not by itself solve China's energy problems. But together with energy efficiency and the cleaner and more-efficient use of coal, it can make a big difference. The question now is whether China can ramp up its renewable energy development to the point where it puts a serious dent in the nation's dependence on coal and builds the foundation for a cleaner energy economy.

How this story ends up may have as large an impact on the world's future as it does on China's. If China is able to scale up its renewable energy technologies to the levels needed to have an impact domestically, and if it is able to achieve the low prices needed to succeed in the local market (known in manufacturing circles as the "China price"), it may be virtually inevitable that these same technologies will soon be adopted on a massive scale around the globe.

The future of the global climate may rest in large measure on China's ability to lead the world into the age of renewable energy, much as the United States led the world into the age of oil roughly a century ago.

—*Christopher Flavin, President,*
Worldwatch Institute

Summary

China's need for secure, affordable, and environmentally sustainable energy for its 1.3 billion people is palpable. In 2006, China's energy use was already the second highest in the world, having nearly doubled in the last decade, and its electricity use is growing even faster, having doubled since 2000. With both energy-intensive industry and high-tech manufacturing, China now serves as factory to the world. Rising living standards also mean more domestic consumption, including high-energy-use items like air conditioners and cars. By 2020, annual vehicle sales in China are expected to exceed those in the United States.

While most of China's electricity comes from coal and hydropower, the growing use of oil for China's burgeoning vehicle fleet is adding greatly to concerns about energy security. Already, China must import nearly half of its oil. Concerns about energy security, power capacity shortages, and air pollution are all adding urgency and pressure to switch to alternative technologies and fuels, including greater energy efficiency, "clean coal" technologies, nuclear power, and renewable energy. Climate change also adds pressure—China will soon pass the United States as the largest emitter of carbon dioxide from fossil fuels.

China has become a global leader in renewable energy. It is expected to invest more than $10 billion in new renewable energy capacity in 2007, second only to Germany. Most of this is for small hydropower, solar hot water, and wind power. Meanwhile, investment in large hydropower continues at $6–10 billion annually. A landmark renewable energy law, enacted in 2005, supports continued expansion of renewables as a national priority. China currently obtains 8 percent of its energy and 17 percent of its electricity from renewables— shares that are projected to increase to 15 percent and 21 percent by 2020.

Among renewable energy sources:

- **Wind power** is the fastest-growing power-generation technology in China, having doubled in capacity during 2006 alone. While wind is still slightly more expensive than coal power, policies encourage competitive pressure on costs, and new mandates require power companies to obtain a minimum share of their power from wind and other renewables. China is home to more than 50 aspiring domestic manufacturers of wind turbines and a number of foreign producers.

- **Solar power** is still in its infancy in China, although a growing amount is used in rural areas and other off-grid applications. A large market for grid-tied solar photovoltaic (PV) is still several years away, once costs decline further. Already, China is a global manufacturing powerhouse for solar PV, third only to Japan and Germany, with huge investments in recent years and much more expected.

- China is the world's largest market for **solar hot water**, with nearly two-thirds of global capacity. The country's 40 million solar hot water systems mean that more than 10 percent of Chinese households rely on the sun to heat their water. When Chinese firms eventually turn to exporting, the lower costs of their units—seven times less than in Europe—could affect markets globally.

- **Biomass power** in China comes mostly from sugarcane wastes and rice husks, and has not grown in recent years. New policies will likely

Summary

mean more biomass power from other sources, such as agricultural and forestry wastes. In addition, industrial-scale biogas, such as from animal wastes, is starting to make a contribution to power generation.

• **Biofuels for transportation** have received widespread attention in China. Ethanol is produced in modest amounts from corn, and biodiesel is produced in small amounts from waste cooking oil. The government plans to expand biofuels production from cassava, sweet sorghum, and oilseed crops, although the large-scale potential is limited. The greatest promise lies with cellulosic ethanol, which many expect to become commercially viable within 7–10 years. If China could use its vast cellulosic resource of agricultural and forestry wastes—up to half a billion tons per year—it might become a major ethanol producer after 2020.

It is likely that China will meet and even exceed its renewable energy development targets for 2020. Total power capacity from renewables could reach 400 gigawatts by 2020, nearly triple the 135 gigawatts existing in 2006, with hydro, wind, biomass, and solar PV power making the greatest contributions. More than one-third of China's households could be using solar hot water by 2020 if current targets and policies are continued. Use of other renewables, including biogas and perhaps solar thermal power, will increase as well.

Achieving these outcomes will depend on domestic industry development, the availability of skilled personnel, technology cost reductions, continued aggressive government policy, appropriate pricing levels, and allowance for distributed power generation by electric utilities. Given China's strong commitment to becoming a world leader in renewables manufacturing, as well as concerns about energy security, power shortages, air pollution, and climate change, the future of renewable energy in China appears bright.

This report is a product of Worldwatch's China Program and was made possible through the support of the Blue Moon Fund. The China Program aims to bridge the perspectives of Worldwatch researchers with the expertise of researchers in China and to provide accurate, accessible, and timely information to the widest audience possible. For additional analysis on China's sustainable development, visit the Institute's *China Watch* news service at www.worldwatch.org/taxonomy/term/53.

China's Energy Crossroads

When *Forbes Magazine* published its annual list of the world's billionaires in 2006, there were more Chinese on the list than ever before. More surprising was the name that topped the national list. One might have expected the richest person in China to be the chief executive of a recently privatized steel company, or perhaps an investor in one of the giant trading firms or software companies that have sprung up in the country. And if the newly minted billionaire were in the energy business, it would be natural to expect him to be a baron of coal, the country's dominant energy source. Instead, the Bill Gates of China turned out to be Shi Zhengrong, a little-known scientist and founding CEO of a small solar company that had just gone public the year before.[1]*

Wealth creation is often a leading economic indicator, signaling where an economy is headed rather than where it is today. John D. Rockefeller became the richest American by dominating the oil industry well before the widespread use of automobiles began, and Bill Gates took that title long before most Americans had personal computers. Shi Zhengrong's company, Suntech Power Holdings Ltd., has experienced a similarly meteoric rise—topping all U.S. competitors to become the world's fourth-largest producer of solar cells only a few years after beginning production.[2] Founded with just 20 employees in 2002, Suntech now claims a market value of more than $6 billion.[3]†

Although virtually all of Suntech's products are exported, leaving coal at the commanding heights of China's energy industry, the dramatic emergence of this renewable energy powerhouse in the world's fastest-growing economy carries a symbolic significance with global implications. The use of renewable energy is undergoing unprecedented worldwide growth—with over $50 billion invested during 2006—and China is poised to lead continued growth in the decade ahead.[4]

China's need for secure, affordable, and environmentally sustainable energy for its 1.3 billion people is palpable. Indeed, China's leaders frequently describe meeting the energy needs of their booming economy as one of the principal economic development challenges facing the nation. In 2006, China's energy use was already the second highest in the world,

Steel mills blow smoke over residential buildings in Benxi, one of China's most polluted cities.

© Gilles Sabrie/Corbis

---

* Endnotes are grouped by section and begin on page 37.

†All dollar amounts are expressed in U.S. dollars unless indicated otherwise.

having increased 75 percent in the last decade.[5] (See Figure 1.) This rapid growth reflects the fact that China has embarked on the most energy-intensive stage of its development—effectively entering the industrial age and the information age simultaneously. And China is not only meeting the rapidly growing needs of its own people for services like transportation, refrigeration, and hot water; it is also serving as factory to the world, using large amounts of energy to make goods that are consumed abroad. Never in history have the energy needs of a large country grown so rapidly.

Despite its surging energy demand, China's per-capita energy use is still far below that of industrial countries. In 2006, it reached 1.3 tons of oil equivalent (toe), compared to 4.2 toe in Japan and 7.9 toe in the United States.[6*] However, urban dwellers in China use nearly three times more electricity and commercial energy per person than rural residents do, and the nation's urban population has grown rapidly, from 375 million in 1999 to 577 million in 2006.[7] This massive rural-to-urban transition continues today, adding tens of millions of people to China's cities each year and driving up national energy use.

Seventy percent of China's primary energy comes from coal, compared with less than 25 percent in the United States and Japan.[8] Coal is used to satisfy a wide range of domestic energy needs, including electricity and heating, and it is a key driver of the nation's industrial development. Coal also provides energy security to China—which has many decades of reserves—and is less expensive than other energy sources.

The booming electric power industry is responsible for most of the surge in China's coal use in the past five years. Coal alone currently provides 80 percent of the nation's electricity.[9] Chinese electricity demand doubled between 2000 and 2006, catching the nation's power industry by surprise.[10] Since 2003, the country has faced electricity shortages and frequent blackouts in many

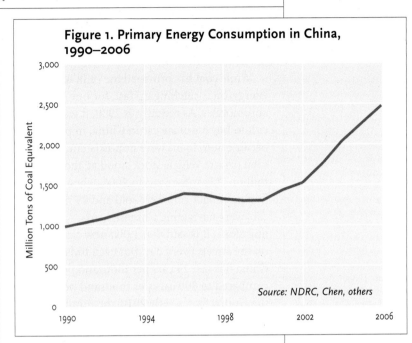

Figure 1. Primary Energy Consumption in China, 1990–2006

Million Tons of Coal Equivalent

Source: NDRC, Chen, others

provinces. The electric utility industry responded by adding 66 gigawatts (GW) of generating capacity in 2005 and 101 GW in 2006—equal to the total capacity of France and more than any country has ever added in a single year.[11] This represents the addition of more than two 600-megawatt coal power plants every week. Power prices are rising in order to finance the construction of power plants, transmission lines, and environmental controls—and to pay for the rising price of the coal that fuels most of the new plants.[12]

Total electricity generating capacity in China reached 620 GW in 2006, compared with about 1,100 GW in the United States and 730 GW in the European Union.[13] While coal is the backbone of China's power sector, the country also has almost 130 GW of hydropower.[14] When the mammoth Three Gorges dam becomes fully operational in 2009, it will add 18 GW of capacity and produce 85 billion kilowatt-hours (kWh) of electricity annually—equivalent to the electricity consumed by 50 million urban Chinese households.[15] Several other large hydro projects are in progress, among them the 6 GW Xiangjiaba plant on the upper reaches of the Yangtze River, scheduled for completion by 2015.[16] Nuclear power provides just 7 GW of China's electric capacity, and despite ambitious con-

---

*Units of measure throughout this report are metric unless common usage dictates otherwise.

struction plans, it is unlikely to provide more than 5 percent of the country's electricity in the next few decades.[17]

While coal has provided the bulk of China's energy, oil is catching up fast, for one reason: automobiles. As recently as 2000, it was difficult to buy a private car in China, in part because auto loans were non-existent, and the total private vehicle stock stood at about 10 million.[18] Fast-forward to 2006, when 4 million passenger cars were sold and 29 million cars were navigating Chinese roads.[19] In Beijing alone, it is said that 1,000 new cars appear on the streets every day. But even today, China has just 24 cars per thousand people, compared to 800 cars per thousand people in the United States.[20] By 2010, the number of cars in China is expected to swell to over 50 million, and by 2020 annual vehicle sales in the country are expected to exceed those in the United States.[21]

Consequently, the country's use of oil is booming. In 2006, China consumed 7.4 million barrels of oil each day, double the 1996 level and second only to the United States.[22] Nearly half of this oil (46 percent) was imported, up from only 31 percent in 2000.[23] Since domestic reserves are relatively modest, Chinese oil production is expected to grow only slowly and could begin to decline as early as 2020.[24] With global oil reserves also limited, the question of how to fuel China's rapidly growing transportation system could have a profound effect on the global oil market and on virtually every other economy on the planet.

China's frenzied energy development has produced environmental problems of unprecedented magnitude, many of them related to the country's heavy dependence on coal. According to one estimate, only 1 percent of the 577 million urban Chinese breathe air that meets European Union air-quality standards.[25] Chinese air contains high quantities of several pollutants that are hazardous to human health as well as to crops and forests—including sulfur dioxide, ozone, and particulate matter. Average particulate levels in Beijing, China's capital, are 141 micrograms per cubic meter of air, compared with maximum safety standards of 50 micrograms in the United States and 40 micrograms in the European Union.[26]

In addition, toxic metals such as mercury are building up in water supplies and on agricultural fields throughout China. A 2004 study estimated that pollution was reducing the country's gross domestic product (GDP) by 3 percent—a figure that other scholars believe is an underestimate.[27] Much of the burden is being borne by Chinese citizens. An unpublished World Bank study in 2007 concluded that poor air quality is causing between 350,000 and 400,000 premature deaths in the country each year.[28]

China's air pollution is rapidly becoming a regional and global problem as well. Acid rain and enormous clouds of "brown haze," composed mainly of particulate matter, threaten populations and ecosystems throughout Asia, particularly in Japan and Korea.[29] Even as far away as North America, a significant share of the toxic mercury that falls from the air originates in China. On some days in Los Angeles, nearly one-quarter of the particulate matter in the air is thought to be of Chinese origin.[30]

China is also on its way to becoming the world's largest contributor to global climate change. The country's total emissions of carbon dioxide (CO_2) will soon exceed those of the United States, even as its per-capita emissions are about one-sixth those of the United States.[31] Chinese per-capita emissions are roughly 3 tons, compared with 10 tons in Japan and 20 tons in the United States.[32] China's CO_2 emissions are growing rapidly, however—at close to 10 percent annually.* In June 2007, the government released a report recognizing climate change as a critical national and global challenge.[33] The report pointed to several national initiatives aimed at slowing the growth in carbon emissions and promised more in the years ahead, including greater use of renewable energy.

---

* China's CO_2 emissions are not growing as fast as its energy use, but almost as fast.

To cope with its air pollution and emissions problems, China is beginning to require electric utilities to incorporate "end-of-pipe" emission controls on most new power plants, including flue-gas desulfurization and electrostatic precipitators that remove particulates from smokestack emissions. The government has also mandated the shutdown of thousands of small, inefficient coal-fired power plants, particularly in rural areas, in favor of larger, more-efficient plants that average roughly 600 megawatts each. And researchers across China are working on the "next generation" of clean-coal power plants, such as integrated gasification combined-cycle (IGCC) and "supercritical" power plants, along with large-scale fluidized-bed combustion boilers. Government-funded demonstrations of such plants are planned by 2010, with commercial plants expected in the following decade.[34]

To sustain its rapid pace of economic development while mitigating the impacts of rising energy use, China is pursuing a wide range of new energy options. At the top of the list are improving the efficiency of energy conversion and use and transitioning to renewable energy sources. As in most countries, energy efficiency has advanced with Chinese industrialization as the country has adopted new technologies and developed less-energy-intensive light industries and services. China's energy intensity (the amount of energy required to produce one yuan of national income) fell by 30 percent between 1995 and 2004.[35] (See Figure 2.) Without this improvement, the nation's energy consumption would be 30 percent higher today—a difference equivalent to Japan's total energy use.[36]

China's leaders recognize the strategic importance of improving national energy efficiency, and the country's 11th Five-Year Plan aims to increase efficiency by 20 percent between 2006 and 2010—a rate of improvement of 4 percent per year.[37] This is to be accomplished through a set of specific reductions in energy intensity and improvements in equipment efficiencies.

Among the policies being counted on to achieve the national energy efficiency target are: tightening existing energy-saving regulations and standards; developing comprehensive resource planning and demand-side management in the electric power sector; regulating the scale of energy-intensive and pollution-intensive industries; formulating preferential policies for energy-saving products; and strengthening the development and dissemination of energy conservation technologies.

For example, the government has directed that the efficiency of pumps and fans should improve from a typical 75–80 percent in 2000 to 80–87 percent by 2010.[38] Similarly, coal-fired industrial boilers should improve from a typical 65 percent efficiency to 70–80 percent by 2010.[39] Plans also call for improvements in the energy intensity of key materials by 2020, relative to 2000 levels. For example, the energy needed per ton of steel should decline from 906 kilograms of coal equivalent (kgce) to 700

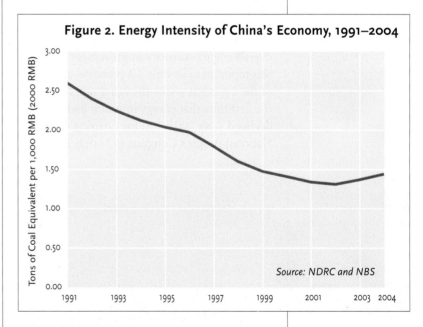

Figure 2. Energy Intensity of China's Economy, 1991–2004

Tons of Coal Equivalent per 1,000 RMB (2000 RMB)

Source: NDRC and NBS

kgce; for aluminum from 9.9 tons of coal equivalent to 9.2 tons; and for cement from 181 kgce to 129 kgce.

Together, these measures represent one of the most comprehensive energy conservation policies in the world. But they are also extraordinarily difficult to implement. Across China, the headlong rush for economic development has led private industry and local officials to

A concerto of traditional agriculture and 21st-century energy technology, Tongyu Tongfa Wind Farm, Jilin.

© Greenpeace/Hu Wei. Photo courtesy of Li Junfeng.

circumvent regulations that would raise costs or slow the pace of construction. In 2006, the overall energy-intensity improvement in China was reported to be only 1.4 percent—far short of the 4 percent goal—though it represented the first time that energy intensity had declined since 2003.[40] At the opening of the National People's Congress in March 2007, government officials acknowledged the failure and vowed to redouble their efforts.[41] In the first half of 2007, the reduction in energy intensity accelerated, and energy intensity was 2.8 percent lower compared with the same period the previous year, due mainly to industrial efficiency improvements.[42]

The Promise of Renewables

In June 2004, the German Government hosted an international meeting of energy leaders— dubbed "Renewables 2004"— intended to launch a renewed global push for renewable energy.[1] Amid the diplomatic speeches and glitzy corporate displays, one side-event to the large conference in the former German parliament hall stood out: a group of senior Chinese officials had flown in from Beijing to announce an ambitious national commitment to renewable energy, including the goal of obtaining 16 percent of the country's energy from renewables by 2020.[2*] Several hundred international energy officials and experts squeezed into a large meeting room to hear the announcement— many of them impressed by China's ambition, but skeptical that its goals would be met.

Three frenetic years after that gathering in Bonn, China's policy machinery for renewable energy is in high gear and its renewables sector is booming, presenting a picture that is far more diverse, fast changing, and complex than any of the luminaries assembled in 2004 could have imagined. China has already become a global leader in renewable energy, and it is poised to hold this lead. In total, some $9–10 billion was invested in new renewable energy capacity in China in 2006 (excluding large hydropower), and investment in 2007 is likely to exceed $10 billion.[3]

China currently gets 8 percent of its primary energy and 17 percent of its electricity from renewable sources, mostly large hydro-

power.[4] (See Table 1.) Given that domestic energy consumption is expected to almost double by 2020, the government's goal of doubling the renewable energy share to 15 percent means that the absolute amount of renewable energy will more than triple. Some experts anticipate that this target could be exceeded, and that the share will keep rising beyond 2020. In October 2006, four renewable energy industry associations announced a common goal to envision and work toward a 25 percent share of renewable energy in China by 2025.[5]

China's overall renewable energy target of 15 percent by 2020 (revised from the previ-

Table 1. Renewable Energy Shares of Electricity and Primary Energy in China, 2006 and Estimates for 2020

		2006 actual		2020 estimated	
Electricity (terrawatt-hours)	Renewables	490	17% share	1,300	21% share
	Total	2,830		6,400	
Primary energy (mtce*)	Renewables	200	8% share	680	15% share
	Total	2,467		4,500	

*million tons of coal equivalent   Source: See Endnote 4 for this section.

ously announced 16 percent) is not far short of the European Union's target of obtaining 12 percent of its energy from renewables by 2010 and 20 percent by 2020.[6] China has also established comprehensive targets for individual renewable energy technologies, such as wind and solar power, solar hot water, and biofuels.[7] (See Table 2.) If all renewable energy targets are met, China should have over 360 gigawatts (GW) of renewable power capacity by 2020, compared to total expected power capacity of 1,000–1,200 GW.[8] The government's goal is to

---

*The 16 percent target was subsequently revised to 15 percent in the final development plan announced in September 2007.

Table 2. China Renewable Energy Targets by Technology, 2010 and 2020

	2006 actual	2010 target	2020 target
Total hydropower (gigawatts)	130	190	300
Small hydropower (gigawatts)	47	60	85
Wind power (gigawatts)	2.6	5	30
Biomass power (gigawatts)	2.0	5.5	30
Solar PV (gigawatts)	0.08	0.3	1.8
Solar hot water (million square meters)	100	150	300
Ethanol (million tons)	1	2	10
Biodiesel (million tons)	0.05	0.2	2
Biomass pellets (million tons)	~0	1	50
Biogas and biomass gasification (billion cubic meters)	8	19	44

Source: See Endnote 7 for this section.

develop a world-class renewable energy industry that is at the cutting-edge of technology development.[9]

To achieve these goals, China's State Council and National People's Congress approved a comprehensive law in February 2005 for developing and promoting renewable energy.[10] The so-called "Renewable Energy Law" provides basic principles, which were then followed by detailed implementing regulations drafted by several related governmental commissions and ministries. The law is intended to meet five overriding goals: (1) establish the importance of renewable energy in China's national energy strategy; (2) remove market barriers; (3) create markets for renewable energy; (4) set up a financial guarantee system; and (5) create awareness, skills, and understanding.

At its core, the Renewable Energy Law is designed to establish a framework of responsibility, requiring the national government to formulate development targets, strategic plans, and financial-guarantee measures for renewable energy. The law also establishes a framework for sharing the extra costs of renewable energy among designated segments of consumers, and creates economic incentives and penalties to motivate companies to act consistently with plans and targets. In addition, it provides a long-term development plan, government research and development (R&D), resource surveys, technology standards, and

building codes for integrating solar hot water into new construction.

This groundbreaking law has its roots in decades of planning for renewables. In the 1980s, the State Council issued "Recommendations on Promoting the Development of Rural Energy," which made renewable energy part of rural energy development plans. As renewable energy power-generation technologies matured, in 1994 the Ministry of Power issued "Recommendations on the Construction and Management of Wind Farms," establishing a firm foundation for development. This was followed in 1999 by "Policy Recommendations on Promoting the Development of Renewable Energy," which made further progress in removing barriers to renewable energy. These policies also provided financial support for renewables, including tax incentives, preferential pricing, and credit guarantees.

The new Renewable Energy Law took effect at the start of 2006. One of its key provisions requires power utilities to purchase power from renewable-energy generators—an obligation that formerly did not exist. The law also stipulates a national cost-sharing mechanism whereby power consumers must pay for the extra (incremental) costs of renewable power.[11] And the law establishes fixed premium prices (often called "feed-in tariffs") and pricing mechanisms for biomass and wind power.

For biomass, the law stipulates a 0.25 RMB (3.2 U.S. cent) per kilowatt-hour (kWh) feed-in tariff premium that is added to province-specific average coal tariffs. This premium has resulted in biomass feed-in tariffs typically of 0.55 to 0.60 RMB (about 7 U.S. cents) per kWh, which is considered sufficient to attract private investment. The same implementing regulations specify a quasi-feed-in "government-guided price" for wind power that is influenced by the results of competitive bidding under a parallel "concession" policy. (See Sidebar 1, p. 18.)

The concession policy has also been an important mechanism for promoting wind power since 2003. It establishes a fixed amount of wind power to be bid each year, and then accepts competitive bids from qualified companies, awarding the capacity to the winner based on a number of evaluation criteria, including price. The policy requires the power utilities to pay for the costs of transmission interconnections, an important provision for reducing the costs to project developers. Beyond the national concession policy, several provincial initiatives have already taken hold, and more are expected. Gansu province was the first to enact such policies, in 2006, with a tender for 150 megawatts (MW) of wind farms.[12]

The Renewable Energy Law also specifies that a "mandated market share" of renewable power should be required of the major national generating companies. This means each of these companies must generate or purchase specific shares of their total power from renewable sources. In September 2007, the exact mandated shares were announced as part of the finalized "Medium and Long-Term Development Plan for Renewable Energy in China."[13] According to the plan, the share of non-hydro renewables should reach 1 percent of total power generation by 2010 and 3 percent by 2020 for regions served by centralized power grids. In addition, any power producer with capacity greater than 5 GW must increase its actual ownership of power capacity from non-hydro renewables to 3 percent by 2010 and 8 percent by 2020.

The Chinese government has also reduced value-added taxes (VAT) and income taxes for renewable power technologies. VAT is reduced from its normal 17 percent to 6 percent for small hydro, 8.5 percent for wind power, and 13 percent for biogas power generation.[14] Income taxes are reduced from 33 percent to 15 percent for wind power and biogas power projects. Imported wind turbine components, assemblies, and fully assembled turbines also receive favorable customs duties or are exempt from customs duties if they are classified as "high-tech." Other power-generation technologies may receive similar treatment, but duties vary according to individual circumstances. In

addition, a special fund established by the Ministry of Finance will provide investment subsidies for power generation, although the amounts have not been determined.[15]

Direct R&D spending on renewables is administered through the Ministry of Science and Technology and the National Develop-

Rooftop solar hot water systems in Kunming, Yunnan province.
© U.S. National Renewable Energy Laboratory/NREL

ment and Reform Commission (NDRC), as well as local governments. R&D spending in the 10th Five-Year Plan (2001–05) reached 1 billion RMB over the five years, equivalent to $25 million per year.[16] In addition, the Renewable Energy Law establishes financial support for R&D through a special renewable energy fund administered by the Ministry of Finance. Funds are expected for technology management, training, equipment certification, inspection, and other technical functions.

China's growing commitment to renewable energy is already visible in the marketplace. By the end of 2006, China was in second place globally in total annual investment in renewables, trailing only Germany.[17] The United States ranked third, at about $5 billion, followed by Spain and Japan. Chinese companies have installed more solar water heaters than the rest of the world combined, and governments at all levels are integrating solar hot water into building codes and standards. Indeed, the national government was poised in 2007 to make solar hot water heaters mandatory in all new construction nationwide.[18]

Thanks to its large hydropower sector, China also leads the world in installed renewable power capacity. China had about 135 GW of renewable power capacity in 2006 (including large hydropower), providing 17 percent of the country's electricity.[19] Small hydropower—defined in China as installations less than 50 MW in size—reached 47 GW in 2006, almost doubling from 25 GW in 2000, and has been attracting over $4 billion per year in new investment from a variety of private and public firms engaged in hundreds of projects along China's waterways.[20] Historically, much of the small hydro was used to power county-level power grids in western China that were gradually integrated into provincial-level and national grids.

China is also ranked first in biogas development and production—developed in rural areas with government support.[21] In 2006, China had 2 GW of biomass power capacity.[22] The government is also providing growing support for biofuels for transportation and for innovative biomass technologies for rural households and small industry.

Other advanced renewable technologies in China include a booming wind industry, which is manufacturing an ever-growing share of its state-of-the-art wind turbines domestically. The amount of wind power being installed has doubled in each of the past two years.[23] As a result, China was the world's fifth-largest installer of wind turbines in 2006, with total installed capacity reaching 2.6 GW at the end of the year.[24] That same year, China's booming solar-cell industry became the world's third-largest producer behind Japan and Germany—exporting most of the units to Europe and the United States.[25]

In just a few years, renewable energy has become a strategic priority for China's government and a lucrative investment opportunity for its private sector. The country is extraordinarily well positioned to further strengthen its position as a world leader in a sector that is growing globally at rates above 20 percent annually.[26] China's first advantage is that its market for new energy supplies is more than double that of any other country, creating uniquely large and lucrative markets.

In addition, China's expansive and diverse geography provides it with a rich array of renewable resources, such that the growth of wind, solar, and other technologies will not be resource-constrained for many decades. China also has the advantage of being the world's largest manufacturer of a wide array of industrial and consumer products—and at very low costs compared to industrialized countries. These same capacities and skills will be needed to drive down the cost of renewable energy to make it competitive with fossil fuels.

Wind Power

Wind power is the fastest-growing power-generation technology in China, with existing capacity doubling during 2006 alone.[1] (See Figure 3.) That year, developers installed a total of 1,450 wind turbines, with a combined capacity of 1.3 gigawatts (GW). This was still a small share of the 15 GW of global installations, however, and China was only number five in added capacity behind Germany, Spain, the United States, and India.[2]

In 2007, wind power capacity additions in China were expected to exceed 2 GW.[3] Early in the year, developers ordered an additional 8 GW of turbines for future installation, and about 200 project development companies were actively pursuing or implementing projects.[4] Recent trends mean that the national target of 5 GW of wind power capacity by 2010 will likely be exceeded by 2–3 GW.

Most wind power projects in China are financed through domestic debt and equity finance, with very little foreign participation.[5] Wind power development now proceeds through two separate but interconnected avenues.[6] (See Sidebar 1, p. 18.) The first is the government's "concession" policy of annually awarding competitively bid blocks of capacity to be installed by both private and state-owned project developers. The second is private development through individually negotiated projects, with prices determined on a case-by-case basis by provincial pricing bureaus. In this second case, prices are "guided" by the results of the concession bidding, according to the 2005 national Renewable Energy Law and its implementing regulations.

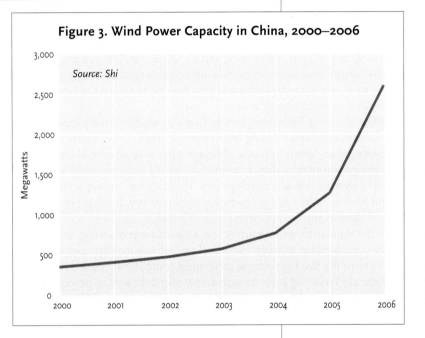

Figure 3. Wind Power Capacity in China, 2000–2006

Source: Shi

Wind power resources in China are especially plentiful in the deserts and plains of the northwest provinces and Inner Mongolia, and in mountain and coastal areas of the southwest and northeast.[7] The provinces and regions that have developed the most wind power so far are Guangdong, Hebei, Inner Mongolia, Jilin, Liaoning, and Xinjiang. Other provinces with good development prospects include Gansu, Ningxia, and Heilongjiang, and the coastal and offshore areas of Shandong, Jiangsu, Zhejiang, Fujian, and Hainan.[8] Among individual cities, Shanghai has taken the most initiative, in part because of its desire to become a manufacturing center for wind turbines. Geographic wind resources should not constrain wind power development in China for decades.

The China Meteorology Research Institute estimates the nation's land-based wind

Sidebar 1. Wind Power Concessions and Private Financing

The Chinese government's "concession" policy for wind power began in 2003. In the first two years, six separate wind power projects were awarded in two rounds of bidding, with a total capacity of 850 megawatts (MW). Bidding continued in 2005 with three more projects with a total capacity of 650 MW, and in 2006 with another three projects totaling 1,000 MW. Altogether, total capacity from the four rounds of bidding during 2003–06 could reach 2,500 MW if all of the capacity bid is actually installed.

Awarded power prices for the concessions were in the range of 0.46–0.49 RMB (5.6–6.0 U.S. cents) per kilowatt-hour (kWh) in 2005 (for 3 of 4 projects), and 0.42–0.50 RMB (5.1–6.0 U.S. cents) per kWh in 2006. Many observers have questioned the viability of these tariff levels, stating that projects cannot possibly be profitable at these levels, and either developers will lose money (hindering sustained industry growth) or the awarded projects simply will not be built. Indeed, actual construction lagged far behind bid awards. Virtually no concession-bid projects were yet operating in 2006; the first operational projects were expected to begin coming online during 2007.

Perhaps partly in recognition of pricing problems, the bid evaluation criteria were changed in 2006. Notably, the weighting assigned to price was reduced from 40 percent to 25 percent, making other non-price factors more important to awards. (Price was weighted 100 percent in 2003 and 2004.) So far, Chinese project developers have won all of the concession projects, leaving private foreign developers to pursue individual projects through government-guided prices. Anecdotally, several private foreign developers, when interviewed, have said they do not expect to be able to win in concession bidding because prices are too low, and thus they do not participate.

When the 2005 Renewable Energy Law was enacted, many expected that a feed-in tariff for wind power would be included in the subsequent implementing regulations. Instead, a "government-guided price" based on concession prices was established, surprising many in the industry. Although there was no official reason given for the lack of a feed-in tariff, it was widely regarded that the government wished to nurture domestic industry in the early years, and decided that a very favorable feed-in tariff would hinder domestic industry development. This idea has been questioned by many, given the experience in Europe and elsewhere where feed-in tariffs have led to strong local industry development. Still, many observers expect that policy may eventually favor a feed-in tariff as the industry matures and grows.

In the meantime, private project developers are proceeding according to the "government-guided price" established through concession bidding, through individual project negotiations and approvals. The top developers were Chinese companies, including three of the five big national generating companies. These developers have established relationships with Chinese banks and are typically financing projects with 80 percent debt and 20 percent equity. There has been no shortage of domestic liquidity, with domestic interest rates of 6–7 percent. So far, there is very little private or foreign equity or foreign institutional lending.

China also has 17 Clean Development Mechanism (CDM) projects for wind power, registered under the United Nations Framework Convention on Climate Change. Azure International estimates that carbon credits add approximately 0.06 RMB (0.8 U.S. cents) per kWh to the revenue from such projects. In the future, foreign investors are more likely to be successful in large or technically difficult projects, or in regions specifically encouraging foreign investment, such as the Western provinces, and are most likely to remain minority partners, according to Azure.

Source: See Endnote 6 for this section.

resources at 250 GW and offshore resources at 750 GW.[9] But these estimates apply to a 10-meter hub height; in practice, modern wind turbines have grown much higher, with hub heights now exceeding 30 meters. Since wind speed (and thus energy) increases with distance above the ground, higher hub heights will produce more energy and power. A recent study by the United Nations Environment Programme showed 3,000 GW of wind resources in China at a hub height of 50 meters.[10]

By 2007, China was home to four major Chinese manufacturers of wind turbines, another six foreign subsidiary manufacturers, and more than 40 firms developing prototypes and aspiring to produce turbines commercially.[11] These companies are developing and producing turbines ranging from 600 kilowatts (kW) to 2 megawatts (MW) in size. In general, Chinese firms have not yet caught up to foreign levels of technology development, in part because foreign firms have been reluctant to license their latest technologies. But Chinese firms are working hard to catch up and amass a domestic "homegrown" base of skilled engineers and technologies. Turbine manufacturing in China has accelerated due to an important "localization" provision of the concession program, which requires that 70 percent of the value of turbines installed under the program be manufactured domestically.*

China's primary domestic wind turbine manufacturer, Goldwind, has been aggressively developing new technology and expanding its market. In 2006, the company's market share of annual turbine sales in China by all manufacturers rose to 33 percent.[12] (See Sidebar 2.) However, Goldwind still lags behind its European counterparts in both technology and scale.

Three other Chinese turbine manufacturers had small market shares in 2006: Huarui (6 percent), Zhejiang "Windey" Engineering (1.5 percent), and Dong Fang Steam Turbine Works (0.8 percent).[13] Other Chinese companies have been developing prototypes and installing test turbines. Hunan Xiangdian Electrical Engineering Co. commissioned a 1.3 MW turbine in Liaoning in 2005 and was gearing up for manufacturing. Hunan Xiangdian was one of two major Chinese electrical equipment manufacturers being supported by the government to develop wind turbine technology.[14] Other companies include Harbin Power Plant Equipment Corporation (Harbin PPEC), a major manufacturing of electrical equipment, Harbin Hafei Winwind, Huide Wind Energy Engineering, and the Wind Energy Research Institute of the Shenyang University of Technology. Harbin PPEC claims its turbine was developed independently and is the first turbine produced entirely as Chinese intellectual property without the use of foreign technology licenses.[15]

Several foreign wind manufacturers are also operating in China, including Vestas of Denmark (with a 24 percent market share in 2006), Gamesa of Spain (17 percent), GE of the United States (13 percent), Nordex of Germany (2 percent), and Suzlon of India (1 percent). These firms are bringing new competencies to the Chinese wind market, including technology, finance, marketing, and production scale. Most of these foreign firms have established new production facilities in China in recent years with tens of millions of dollars of new investment into wholly owned manufacturing subsidiaries. Acciona of Spain, a new entrant in the Chinese market, is an exception, and is establishing a 50/50 manufacturing joint venture with a Chinese partner.[16]

Sidebar 2. Wind Turbine Manufacturer Goldwind Leaps Ahead

Since its establishment in 1997, the wind turbine manufacturer Goldwind has played a key role in developing China's wind power industry. By the end of 2006, the company had cumulatively sold nearly 1,500 turbines with total capacity of 1,100 megawatts (MW). Goldwind has also witnessed a rapid rise in its share of China's cumulative wind power capacity, increasing from 5 percent in 2002 to 26 percent in 2006.

Goldwind has taken advantage of the growing wind power market and enjoys a competitive edge in costs and services due to proximity to the local market. However, the company still lags behind European counterparts in both technology and scale. Most of Goldwind's sales are still of 750 kilowatt models, while most state-of-the-art European products have capacities of 2 MW and above. Additionally, most Goldwind turbines use an older "fixed pitch, constant speed" control system, compared with more sophisticated "variable pitch, variable speed" systems. Consequently, Goldwind has intensified efforts at technological innovation, including employing the services of foreign design companies. Following this model, the company tested and installed its first 1.2 MW wind turbine in 2005–06 and was working on 2.5 and 3 MW models.

Goldwind's technology is viewed as an important national asset. This was illustrated in 2006 when Goldwind explored the prospect of an initial public offering (IPO) on a foreign stock exchange. Although many existing Goldwind investors favored an overseas IPO, the Chinese government was resistant to the idea because it might lead to a subsequent buy-out by foreign owners. This was considered unacceptable given the company's leading position in a strategic industry for China. Instead, Goldwind announced in 2007 that it would list on China's domestic stock market.

Source: See Endnote 12 for this section.

Among Chinese wind farm developers, Longyuan is the leader, having developed almost 40 percent of the nation's existing wind power capacity.[17] Close behind is Huaneng, which is also one of China's five major power-generating companies. Other major project developers are Datang, Guohua, Huadian, and

---

* Chinese customs rulings have also recently begun favoring domestic production of wind turbines, with a 3 percent import duty for individual parts, 8 percent for assembled components, and 17 percent for entire preassembled turbines.

Herdsman drives his sheep through He Lan Shan Wind Farm, Ningxia.
© Greenpeace/Hu Wei. Photo courtesy of Li Junfeng.

China Power Investment. Some foreign project developers have also been part of the picture.

One of the big problems facing China's domestic wind industry is the need for operational experience, testing, and redesign cycles. This process can take several years, and U.S. and European manufacturers have a long head start. This means that uncertainties about quality and technical performance will continue to plague Chinese producers for many years unless shortcuts employing foreign expertise can be found.

Because of the apparent lower costs of wind turbine production in China relative to the United States and Europe, domestically produced turbines, even those made by foreign firms, offer cost advantages to imported turbines. This is also true because of favorable import tariffs on components that prevailed in 2006 and 2007: 17 percent for entire pre-assembled turbines, but only 8 percent for assembled components and 3 percent for individual wind turbine parts.

Thus, foreign manufacturers are profiting by establishing joint ventures and wholly owned subsidiaries for turbine manufacturing. Substantial technology and knowledge can be transferred to local Chinese firms and engineers through joint ventures, less so through the wholly owned subsidiaries. Chinese firms are struggling to acquire specialized engineering knowledge, particularly in aerodynamics, blade design, materials, and control systems, and are turning to foreign design firms for contracted design tools and services, rather than to foreign turbine manufacturers.

Solar Power

China's solar energy potential is enormous.[1] Most of the country has solar resources that are far superior to those in Germany and Japan, the two world leaders in solar power use. However, compared to those countries, solar power is still in its infancy in China. In 2006, China had just 80 megawatts (MW) of solar photovoltaic (PV) capacity installed, compared to 7,700 MW globally.[2]

About half of China's capacity is employed in rural off-grid applications, a market that is increasing at around 5–10 MW per year.[3] (See Sidebar 3, p. 22.) The rest is used for communications, industry, and consumer products. Grid-connected (often called "grid-tied") solar PV is still marginal, just a few megawatts.[4] Rural street lighting is another application that shows large promise: in 2006, Beijing installed about 5 MW of solar power for streetlights in surrounding rural areas.[5] In total, China's domestic PV market grew by about 10 MW in 2006.[6]

A large grid-tied market, such as the 1,000 MW installed in Germany in 2006, is still per- haps 5–7 years away in China, as the cost of solar PV declines further and as conventional power costs rise.[7] Solar power is still too expensive, and the huge subsidies required have made the government reluctant to provide them. In countries where solar PV is doing well around the world today, one or more factors are at work: conventional power prices are extremely high (such as in Japan), large subsidies are being provided (such as in the United States), or favorable feed-in tariffs are offered to small solar PV generators (such as in Europe).

Nevertheless, there are promising developments for grid-tied or building-integrated solar PV in China. In 2005, the Shanghai government announced it was considering a "100,000 roofs" initiative that would put solar PV on residential and commercial buildings.[8] (That initiative was on hold as of late 2007, however.) The Jiangsu provincial government is working on the first phases of a 10,000-roof program and has started to discuss a feed-in tariff policy with local utilities.[9] The city of Shenzhen has built a 1 MW grid-tied solar PV

Yang Ba Jing grid-connected solar PV station, Tibet.
© Photo courtesy of Li Junfeng.

plant on its World Garden Expo building.[10] Other exhibition buildings and demonstration projects are being constructed for the Beijing 2008 Olympics and the Shanghai 2010 World Expo.[11] The Beijing site includes a 500-kilowatt (kW) solar PV generating plant and smaller

riveted to the fast growth potential and expansion plans of the Chinese solar PV industry.[12] More than 15 major solar cell manufacturers employed over 20,000 people in 2006, and new companies were appearing monthly during 2007.[13] Solar PV cell production capacity in China jumped from 350 MW in 2005 to over 1,000 MW in 2006, and virtually every player in the industry announced further capacity expansion, some planning to double or triple capacity in just a few years.[14] (See Table 3.) Production capacity was expected to reach 1,500 MW in 2007.[15] These production levels are much higher than domestic demand, so virtually all production is exported. Some believe this could hinder the industry, but others believe that Chinese industry can continue to grow based on exports alone.

Sidebar 3. Electrifying Rural China: The Role of Renewables

Due to intensive rural electrification programs in recent decades, only a small fraction of rural households in China still lack access to electricity. In 2006, an estimated 4 million households remained un-electrified, representing roughly 15 million people. Renewable energy technologies, including household solar PV systems, biogas digesters (see Sidebar 6, p. 29), and solar hot water heaters, have played an important role in providing electricity, heating, and lighting to rural households. By 2006, nearly 1 million "solar home systems" were being used by rural households in China. Such systems are sold through a thriving network of private dealers and installers and typically include a solar panel, storage battery, and lights. A standard 20-watt PV system sells for around 850–1,000 RMB ($115–135).

Other renewable energy systems used in China to provide power to rural households are small wind turbines and micro-hydro systems (smaller than 100 kilowatts). Micro-hydro systems serve about 500,000 rural households. Household-scale wind systems serve about 200,000 rural households, primarily in Inner Mongolia, Xinjiang, Gansu, and Qinghai regions, with an average capacity per household of just 170 watts. In recent years, new "village power" systems have been promoted by the government, often combining solar PV, small hydro, wind power, and sometimes battery storage.

The Chinese government and some local governments have conducted programs and provided investment subsidies for the development of rural renewable energy. These include, for example, a program of subsidies to small-scale PV systems and wind systems in remote areas as well as rural programs for small hydropower and household biogas. During 2001–04, the national "Brightness Program" conducted pilot projects and installed about 30,000 household-scale solar PV systems and 40 village-scale solar PV systems in Inner Mongolia, Gansu, Tibet, Xinjiang, and Qinghai. This was followed by the "Township Electrification Program," which electrified an impressive 300,000 households (1.3 million people) using renewable energy in just two years (2003–04). That program served about 900,000 people in 270 townships with small hydro, and another 350,000 people in 720 townships with PV-only and PV-wind village-scale systems (typically 30–150 kilowatts in size).

Following past programs, the Chinese government in 2006 was planning further village electrification programs through 2015 that would be designed to achieve full rural electrification of remaining un-served populations. However, it appeared that national priority was shifting toward power-grid extension to the remaining un-electrified rural households, rather than use of distributed renewable energy.

Source: See Endnote 3 for this section.

Chinese solar PV companies are becoming very ambitious in their investment and expansion plans. In 2005, Suntech Power Holdings Ltd. started operating a new 150 MW production facility, and the company reached 270 MW of capacity in 2006.[16] (See Sidebar 4, p. 24.) Suntech, which started up only six years ago, is now China's leading manufacturer of solar PV cells, modules, and systems, and has grown into an equal-weight competitor to major Japanese and European producers in international markets. A second company, China Sunergy (formerly Nanjing CEEG PV Tech), is planning new capacity of 600 MW by 2008 and 1,500 MW by 2010.[17] Tianwei Yingli is planning 600 MW by 2008.[18]

solar PV arrays at all entrances of the Olympic National Stadium. Several other smaller demonstrations of building-integrated PV were proceeding in 2006 and 2007.

Led by a number of high-profile initial public stock offerings (IPOs), some valued in the billions of dollars, global attention has been

Total investment by these three companies—Suntech, China Sunergy, and Tianwei Yingli—might exceed 10 billion RMB ($1.3 billion) by the 2008–10 timeframe.[19] Other

Table 3. Planned Additions to Chinese Solar PV Production Capacity, 2007–2010

	Existing Capacity 2006	Planned Additions 2007–10
	(megawatts)	
Suntech	270	500
China Sunergy	190	600
Jiangsu Linyang	100	500
Ningbo	100	100
Baoding Tianwei-Yingli	90	600
Trina Solar	75	500
Solarfun	60	240
Xian Jiayang	50	100
Total (including others)	>1,000	>3,000

Source: See Endnote 14 for this section.

companies entering the picture include Jiangxi LDK Solar Hi-Tech, a wafer manufacturer that has a currently installed capacity of about 100 MW and plans to expand this to 1,000 MW by 2010.[20] Considering all companies and announced plans, some industry observers believe solar PV production capacity in China will reach more than 4,000 MW by 2010, up from 1,000 MW in 2006.[21]

One of the uncertainties for the Chinese solar PV industry is the availability of poly-silicon feedstock. This "silicon shortage" has been much discussed in the industry worldwide since 2004 and is expected to continue through 2008. China had virtually no domestic silicon producers in the earlier years, but in response to the rapid rise of the solar PV industry, new sources of solar-grade silicon are emerging. Chinese silicon production for PV use was about 340 tons in 2006, compared to domestic demand of over 3,000 tons, with the difference being imported.[22] However, over 4,000 tons of new silicon production capacity by several firms was under development and expected to come online in 2007 and 2008.[23]

Chinese solar PV manufacturers seem confident they can out-compete foreign manufacturers. Lower labor costs may play a small part, as some amount of production equipment can be substituted with cheaper manual labor, thus reducing capital equipment costs. Right now, solar PV prices are high due to sup-

PV-powered street-lights in Rizhao.
© Rizhao Municipal Government

Sidebar 4. PV Manufacturer Suntech Gains International Recognition

Suntech Power Holdings Ltd. flipped the switch on its first polycrystalline silicon solar cell assembly line in September 2002. Founded the year before with a $6 million grant from its home city of Wuxi, Suntech's initial production capacity was very modest—just 10 megawatts (MW). Since then, the company's production capacity has rocketed higher, reaching 270 MW in 2006 and expected to hit 470 MW in 2007, making Suntech the world's fourth-largest solar cell maker. Major competitors include Sharp and Kyocera of Japan, and Q-cells of Germany. Suntech is eyeing the year 2010, with production capacity ambitiously projected to reach 1,000 MW, along with a likely ranking among the world's top three solar cell producers.

Suntech is striving to hold a competitive edge among Chinese solar PV manufacturers by emphasizing innovation and the building of technical know-how. Its founder and CEO, Shi Zhengrong, received a doctorate in thin-film solar cell research while studying in Australia. He remained a researcher in Australia long enough to bring back dozens of patented innovations to China, as well as business savvy about the importance of innovation to business growth. Suntech invests 5 percent of its annual revenue back into R&D, and has established a world-class R&D center housing more than 20 senior experts.

In 2006, Suntech set up a second R&D center in nearby Shanghai to attract even more high-quality talent. That facility will focus on thin-film PV, a leading-edge technology that is expected to reduce future solar PV costs substantially. The Shanghai facility also includes a thin-film manufacturing facility, expected to become operational in 2008 and to reach 50 MW of production capacity in 2009.

Suntech became the first private Chinese firm to be listed on the New York Stock Exchange with its initial public offering in December 2005, which saw Suntech's market capitalization soar to $6 billion and pushed Dr. Shi's personal net worth to $2.2 billion. With its economic security, Suntech has been able to plan far ahead and secure future sources of silicon, a critical raw material, amidst a tight global silicon market. In 2006, Suntech signed a $6 billion contract with U.S. silicon wafer giant EMEC to ensure supply for the next 10 years, as well as long-term silicon supply contracts with several other firms.

Paradoxically, almost none of the company's products—some $600 million worth in 2006—are used in China. Solar power is still too expensive domestically, and the government has not provided subsidies or feed-in tariffs for solar PV like those found in the growing solar markets of the United States and Europe. Much of Suntech's output is exported to Spain and Germany. In Germany, households and businesses install the panels on rooftops and collect 37–49 eurocents (48–65 U.S. cents) per kilowatt-hour in revenue—enough to pay for the panels and make a tidy profit.

Source: See Endnote 16 for this section.

ply shortages relative to global demand, but as supply increases and technology improves, prices should start to fall (maybe to $2.50 per watt by 2010, from $3.50 per watt today). As that happens, Chinese competitiveness will be put to the real test.

Chinese firms are freely able to purchase solar PV manufacturing equipment from foreign vendors. They are also working on their own R&D programs. But the Chinese firms are currently so focused on expanding production capacity (at breakneck rates) that technology innovation takes a distant second place in priority. Thus, at present Chinese solar PV firms do not really need technology cooperation

with the United States and Europe. Capital and management expertise (including quality control and marketing) are probably the most important elements presently.

This situation could change if the technology landscape changes in the future and Chinese firms face more pressure to innovate due to new technologies entering the commercial marketplace and lower profit margins from declining prices. Given the current rate of growth of the global solar industry, serious competitive pressure to innovate seems some years distant, unless there is a severe downturn in global demand for solar PV.

Solar Hot Water and Heating

While China has only limited experience with solar power, it is already a global leader in taking advantage of the sun's energy for heating. The country is now the largest market for solar hot water in the world, with nearly two-thirds of total global capacity (excluding systems used to heat swimming pools). Growth has been rapid, rising from 35 million square meters of installed capacity in 2000 to 100 million square meters by the end of 2006.[1]

China added 20 million square meters of new capacity in 2006 alone, for an estimated 40 million solar thermal systems overall.[2] This means that more than 10 percent of Chinese households now rely on the sun to heat their water. In 2005, China avoided nearly 14 million tons of carbon dioxide emissions through its use of solar thermal systems, according to an International Energy Agency report.[3]

Historically, the demand for solar hot water came primarily from China's rural areas, which typically lack central and district heating systems. Solar thermal systems have, for example, enabled farmers to bathe with warm water in the privacy of their homes rather than in cold local streams or communal baths, dramatically improving the quality of life for many.[4] But while rural demand continues, recent growth has been driven mainly by urban installations on existing and new structures, including high-rise apartment buildings.

Today, solar heating systems can be found everywhere in urban China—on homes, apartment and office towers, schools, and hotels—particularly in the southern provinces. In many southern cities, and in some northern ones such as Rizhao, vast "forests" of solar hot water

Solar hot water systems installed on the roof of an apartment building in Rizhao.
© Rizhao Municipal Government

heaters can be seen jostling for space on the rooftops of entire neighborhoods.[5] (See Sidebar 5, p. 26.) By 2005, more than one-third of the national market for the systems was in urban areas, and this share continues to grow.[6]

A typical Chinese system comprises two square meters of vacuum tube collectors, a 180-liter storage tank, and an open circulation system, suitable for warmer regions. Increasingly, the Chinese view solar water heaters as desirable appliances that rank high on their lists of priorities. System costs have fallen dramatically over the years and solar heating is relatively affordable today, thanks to a combination of low-cost labor, cheap materials, and competition among a large number of domestic solar companies.[7]

Chinese companies now produce solar hot water heaters at costs that are one-fifth to one-

Rooftop solar hot water systems in Mengzi Residential Compound, Yunnan province.
© Photo courtesy of Li Junfeng.

Sidebar 5. Rizhao: City of Sunshine

Solar hot water has grabbed Rizhao like no other Chinese city. After 15 years of effort—including provincial subsidies, the political will of local leaders, and local industries that seized the opportunity to advance their products—this city of nearly three million people in Shandong Province can truly claim the meaning of its name, "City of Sunshine" in Chinese. Throughout the city, rooftops or walls of most buildings are covered with solar collectors. In the central district, 99 percent of households get their hot water from the sun, as do more than 30 percent of households in local suburbs and villages. And more than 60,000 local greenhouses stay warm with solar panels.

By 2007, the solar-collecting area of Rizhao totaled more than half a million square meters, saving the energy equivalent of 100,000 tons of coal every year. Technological breakthroughs and economies of scale in production have brought the costs of solar water heaters down to about $190 per unit. The units can be attached easily to buildings and enable owners to save an average of $120 each year in electricity purchases. This is important in a city where average per-capita incomes are below those of most other cities in the region.

Solar panels were initially installed on government buildings and on the homes of city leaders to set an example. The Shandong provincial government invested in the solar thermal industry to help drive innovations. And the municipal government enacted policies to encourage local development. Today, the City of Rizhao mandates that all new buildings incorporate solar panels; projects that do not include solar heaters in their blueprints will not be permitted. The city has enacted regulations to standardize the installation and use of solar panels, and is also using methane gas for some cooking and electricity production.

In addition, the city's leaders see solar energy as a starting point for triggering social, economic, and cultural development through a healthier environment. And their vision appears to be turning to reality. Reduced use of coal has improved the local environment, and Rizhao is consistently ranked as one of the top 10 cities for air quality in China. The cleaner environment is playing a role in drawing foreign direct investment, tourists, and even new university campuses to this coastal city.

Source: See Endnote 5 for this section.

eighth those found in the United States and Europe. In 2002, 70 percent of all solar hot water heaters in China were sold at prices below 1,500 RMB (about $200), which, given typical sizes, comes to about $120 per square meter.[8] (Typical prices in Europe run to $800 a square meter and more.) The most expensive systems, sized 4–6 square meters with forced circulation and electrical backup, cost $300 a square meter.[9]

The Chinese solar hot water industry is fragmented, with only a few major players, and it lacks a strong technology and economic underpinning. However, several prominent household appliance makers, including Haier, Ocma, and Huati (equivalent to a Whirlpool in the United States or a Miele in Germany), have also recently entered the solar hot water market. Retailers and installation services are ubiquitous in China, and there is a large selection of brands, with more than 1,000 manufacturers employing more than 150,000 people throughout the country.[10] In 2005, the industry claimed sales revenue of $2.5 billion.[11]

Most of this growth to date has occurred with minimal government involvement. Increasingly, however, national and local government departments, architects, and real-estate developers are paying attention to solar hot water and working to promote its development and use. In mid-2007 the National Development and Reform Commission (NDRC) issued a "Plan on Enforcement of Utilization of Solar Energy Heating Nationwide" that will soon mandate solar hot water heating in new construction.[12] While detailed regulations are not yet finalized, the mandate is expected to apply to hospitals, schools, and hotels. It is also expected to require new construction to allow space on rooftops for the addition of solar hot water heaters and to encourage retrofits of existing government buildings. In 2006, the booming southern city of Shenzhen mandated solar hot water in all new residential buildings below 12 stories in height.[13]

The Chinese government aims for 150 million square meters of solar water heating systems by 2010 and 300 million square meters by 2020.[14] New policies and building practices mean that the 20–25 percent annual growth rates of recent years should continue for the foreseeable future. And some experts suggest that China could achieve 400 million square meters of installed capacity by 2020 and 800 million square meters by 2030.[15] If such projections come to pass, more than half of all Chinese households could be using solar hot water by 2030.

To meet these targets, domestic production is expected to increase dramatically, rising from 20 million square meters in 2006 to perhaps 30 million square meters before 2020.[16] Some experts estimate that annual production could reach 45 million square meters by 2020, and even more if export markets for Chinese products grow.[17] In addition to hot water, solar-assisted space heating is a relatively new application that is just taking hold in parts of Europe and could become part of China's market as well.[18]

The largest solar hot water manufacturer in the world is Himin Group, located in the city of Dezhou in Shandong province. With 50,000 employees worldwide, Himin produces over 1 million solar hot water systems annually.[19] Most of these are for the Chinese domestic market, but Himin has more recently targeted export markets. The company's products receive national recognition as a top brand, and Himin's president, Huang Ming, was named China's most influential private entrepreneur in 2003.[20]

Technology improvements on a number of fronts will aid in this expansion. Manufacturers are now working to improve the efficiency of heat collection per unit of area of collector to allow for accommodation of more heating capacity on rooftops with limited space. Today, apartment buildings up to 10 stories can reasonably accommodate solar hot water for all residents. But many new urban apartment buildings in China are taller than this. Improvements in collector efficiency, as well as applications on building surfaces other than rooftops alone, will allow application on taller buildings.

Quality improvements and the adoption of national standards are also critical for advancing China's solar heating industry. In 2001 and 2002, the Chinese government developed three new industry standards, which it began implementing in 2002. In 2005, the country established national testing and certification centers. The United Nations Development Programme and the Global Environment Facility have also played a role in industry development. In recent years, they have funded a project that has established standards and testing certifications in China, with three in place by 2006.[21]

Assuming China can overcome challenges associated with system quality, standards, cus-

Rooftop solar hot water systems on a restaurant in Lijiang.
© Photo courtesy of Li Junfeng.

tomization for different national markets, and distribution channels—and there is no reason it cannot—there is enormous potential for it to export its solar thermal systems around the world. If Chinese firms can produce products that meet quality levels and technical standards of foreign markets, and can partner with major retail distribution companies, such as Wal-Mart in the United States, the less-expensive Chinese products may transform foreign markets as well.

Biomass Power and Biofuels

In 2006, China had about 2 gigawatts (GW) of biomass power-generation capacity.[1] Most of this capacity comes from combined heat-and-power (CHP) plants in the sugar industry, with sugarcane waste (bagasse) being the primary feedstock. Rice plantations also use rice waste (husks) in such plants. China's biomass power capacity has not changed appreciably in recent years, though a new generation of biomass power generation is now getting started in two primary categories:

Biomass power plant in Jinzhou, Hebei province. The plant's primary feedstocks are corn and wheat stalks and tree branches.
© Photo courtesy of Li Junfeng.

"industrial-scale" biogas power plants and large-scale power plants that burn a wide variety of agricultural wastes.[2]

Industrial-scale biogas plants in China, typically in the range of 10–100 kilowatts in size, convert industrial and animal wastes into biogas for generating power. There are now more than 1,600 such plants operating in the country, producing more than 8 billion cubic meters of biogas a year, and the future poten-

tial is high.[3] Wastes from agricultural processing and livestock farms could yield 80 billion cubic meters of biogas annually, well above the government's target of 44 billion cubic meters annually by 2020.[4] The government expects 3 GW of power generation from biogas by 2020.[5] In addition to industrial biogas, the government has long made progress with rural household use of biogas in small quantities.[6] (See Sidebar 6.)

The second main category of biomass power generation in China is large-scale combustion of agricultural wastes, typically in a 25-megawatt (MW) size plant.[7] Such a plant can require collection and transport of agricultural waste from a wide area, perhaps even a substantial portion of an entire county. Transport cost typically limits collection distances to within 30–50 kilometers from the plant. Agricultural waste must often be purchased from many different small farmers to supply a single plant. (Crop agriculture in China occurs mainly via small farms; consequently, biomass is often sold in very small quantities and must be aggregated from multiple sellers.)

China's first 25 MW biomass power plant went into commercial operation in 2006 in Shandong province. The plant cost $35 million and burns approximately 150,000–200,000 tons of cotton stalks, tree branches, orchard waste, and forestry waste annually.[8] The ash waste can be used as high-quality potash fertilizer. A few more plants began operation in 2006–07, and the government plans to build another 30 such plants, for a total capacity of perhaps 750 MW.[9]

An estimated 300–350 million tons of agricultural waste could theoretically be available annually nationwide to supply biomass power plants.[10] Estimates for available forestry waste vary greatly, with some in the range of 100–150 million tons per year and one as high as 500 million tons per year.[11] Available forestry wastes are expected to increase in the future due to government tree-planting programs, such as the National Forest Protection Program and the Sloping Cropland Conversion Program.

If a significant share of these agricultural and forestry wastes were to be used for large-scale biomass power plants, a total of 1,000 such plants might be possible, with a total capacity of 25 GW. Higher amounts, up to 50–80 GW, have been analyzed in some scenarios, although it is questionable if such levels, well beyond the government's 2020 target of 30 GW, can be reached.[12] Limitations include competing uses for the wastes, including biomass pellet and briquette production and potentially cellulose-to-ethanol technology when it becomes commercially available.

In addition to biomass for power generation, liquid biofuels for transportation have received widespread attention in China in recent years as alternatives to oil imports.[13] Ethanol, a biofuel derived from sugars and starches, is currently being produced in modest quantities in some parts of the country. Nine provinces now mandate a 10-percent blending of ethanol with all gasoline sold.[14] The 2005 Renewable Energy Law specifically encourages ethanol production. For some years, the national government has provided production subsidies of 1,300 RMB ($170) per ton of ethanol to selected producers, equivalent to about 12 U.S. cents per liter, about the same level of subsidy that ethanol producers receive in the United States.* There are two large Chinese ethanol producers, and total production in 2006 was about 1 billion liters. This compares with global ethanol production of 37 billion liters in 2006, primarily in the United States and Brazil.[15]

---

* Subsidies are limited to certain production levels and apply only to some producers.

Sidebar 6. Household-Scale Biogas and Biomass Pellets for Cooking, Heating, and Lighting

The Chinese government has promoted household biogas digesters, which produce gas from animal and crop wastes, since the 1950s. By 2006, more than 20 million households were using biogas, mainly in stoves for cooking and in lamps for lighting. Current digester use in China represents the equivalent energy of 5 million tons of coal annually, or about 40 million tons of agricultural wastes.

A typical household-scale digester, sized 6–8 cubic meters, produces 300 cubic meters of biogas a year and costs 1,500–2,000 RMB ($200–250), depending on the province. Systems for northern climates are designed to operate inside a greenhouse and tend to be a bit larger. Because digesters are a simple technology, there is no need for advanced expertise, and the units can be supplied by local small companies. Farmers, after receiving training, can build the digesters themselves.

Government subsidies to rural households for constructing new biogas digesters have grown from about 1 billion RMB ($130 million) in 2000 to 2.5 billion RMB ($320 million) in 2006. The subsidy is 800–1,200 RMB ($100–150) per digester. Some estimate that more than 1 million biogas digesters are being produced in China each year, and the government has set targets for 30 million digesters by 2010 and 45 million by 2020. But as rural households become wealthier and reduce their reliance on household animal husbandry, this will affect the viability of household biogas for rural populations.

Biomass pellets are another promising form of energy for rural households. Small-scale pelletizing equipment is just emerging as a commercially viable technology for converting agricultural wastes into compact pellets for stoves and furnaces, as innovations are made in efficiency, cost, and reliability. Government targets for pellets are 1 million tons per year by 2010 and 50 million tons per year by 2020. Pellets can also be used in rural buildings for small combined heat-and-power production, an application common in northern European countries.

Source: See Endnote 6 for this section.

In past years, some of the ethanol produced in China came from rotted (surplus) corn that had accumulated in storage. But by 2006, it was clear that most ethanol was being produced from corn newly obtained from farmers, presumably as the rotted corn stocks were depleted (although some have questioned how big these stocks really were). In mid-2007, China declared a moratorium on expanded ethanol production from corn due to concerns about competition with food supplies.[16] As corn prices rose in China in 2007, this translated into higher meat prices due to higher costs for animal feeds, including soybeans. (This was similarly true in North American corn and soy markets due to the huge expansion of ethanol production in the United States in recent years.)

With the 2007 corn-based ethanol moratorium, further expansion of Chinese ethanol production will depend on dedicated plantations. Biofuel plantations are explicitly called for in the 2005 national Renewable Energy Law. In 2007, the government announced it would focus attention on sweet sorghum and cassava plantations as the main feedstocks for ethanol.[17] Sweet sorghum is currently not yet planted on a large scale in China. One estimate shows that the crop could potentially cover more than 600,000 hectares, producing perhaps 3 billion liters of ethanol per year.[18] Cassava, meanwhile, is grown largely in Guangxi and Guangdong provinces, with estimated potential there ranging from 1 to 5 billion liters of ethanol per year.[19] In southern China, some cassava is being imported and the government has waived import duties. Sugar cane is another potential energy crop that could be used for ethanol, with some estimates of potential up to 1.7 billion liters per year.[20]

Beyond sorghum, cassava, and sugar cane, the prospects for significant ethanol expansion in China rest on the future of cellulose-to-ethanol technology. Most experts expect the viability of this technology to be proven within the next 10 years, perhaps even before 2015.[21] Indeed, construction of several cellulosic ethanol plants (based on corn stover or wood waste) is already under way in the United States.[22] And pilot cellulosic ethanol plants are expected in China in the coming years.[23]

The most promising source of ethanol in China is the annual flow of agricultural wastes, which represents a huge cellulose feedstock. Currently, this waste is often left in the field (where at least some of it is needed for fertil-

Using biogas to cook and boil water in Rizhao.
© Rizhao Municipal Government

ization) or is used for animal fodder, household cooking, and other rural applications. As noted earlier for biomass power, such feedstocks could amount to 300–350 million tons per year of agricultural waste and 100–150 million tons per year of forestry wastes. If half of that waste, perhaps 250 million tons per year total, were devoted to cellulosic ethanol, up to 90 billion liters of ethanol per year could be produced.[24] For comparison, Chinese consumption of gasoline in 2006 was 70 billion liters.[25]

A second biofuel, biodiesel, can be produced from waste vegetable oils or oilseed plantations. Currently, the amount of biodiesel produced in China is small and is derived mainly from waste cooking oil.[26] There is a large potential supply of such waste oil if it can be collected and processed cheaply enough into fuel. According to one estimate, up to 4 billion liters per year of biodiesel could be produced from waste cooking oil in China.[27] There is also potential for producing biodiesel from oilseed crops, the cheapest of which is *Jatropha curcas*, which might yield 7 billion liters per year nationwide.[28] Other oilseed crops considered economically viable are Chinese pistachio, yellowhorn, and Wilson's dogwood.

Other potential biodiesel feedstocks include soybeans, peanuts, rapeseeds, cottonseed, and sunflower, although all of these are food crops that are in high demand in China.[29] Rapeseed, for example, can command higher prices as a cooking oil today, but it might become viable for biodiesel within the next decade. The theoretical potential is quite high: one study estimates that 29 million hectares could be planted with rapeseed, producing 21 billion liters of biodiesel annually.[30] A wide variety of pilot efforts to convert various oilseed crops to biodiesel are ongoing in several provinces. Palm oil is another feedstock common in Southeast Asia, and some small Chinese biodiesel producers have started to import palm oil.[31]

Estimates of the long-term biofuels potential in China vary widely. The Chinese Renewable Energy Industries Association calculates that energy crops could yield more than 60 billion liters of liquid fuel per year, including 35 billion liters of ethanol and 27 billion liters of biodiesel.[32] The China Energy Research Institute has estimated that China could produce 19 billion liters of biofuels per year by 2020 and up to 40 billion liters per year by 2030.[33] Other estimates have put the range at 10–30 billion liters by 2020. Most of these estimates go beyond China's national target for ethanol production of 13 billion liters of ethanol and 2.3 billion liters of biodiesel per year by 2020.[34]

Future prospects for biofuels in China will depend on oil prices, the pace of technology development, and the viability and availability of land for large-scale plantation crops. Plantation crops may prove too expensive in the short term, or at least until oil prices increase further. There are also serious concerns about environmental degradation, water resources, and competition for land arising from biofuels plantations.[35] For example, tropical deforestation is occurring in Indonesia and Malaysia to clear land for oil palm plantations, and competition can arise from the use of forest land to plant jatropha. Other indirect environmental effects include the use of biomass for fuel that might otherwise be used to produce heat or electricity, thereby offsetting coal consumption and reducing local air pollution as well as carbon dioxide emissions from coal.[36]

Much of the future of biofuels in China will hinge on the commercial viability of using cellulosic material, particularly agricultural wastes, to produce ethanol, which is not expected before 2015 (although some optimistic forecasts are suggesting 2010–12 is possible). Prospects for cellulose-to-ethanol also depend on the scale of commercial plants relative to the diffuse nature of agricultural waste. The prospects are good that China could get 10–20 percent of its transportation fuels from biofuels by 2020 or 2030. This compares with an International Energy Agency advanced-technology scenario that shows the world getting 3–25 percent of its transportation fuels from bio-based sources by 2050.[37]

Future prospects for biofuels also depend on China's other options for reducing oil imports. These include converting coal into liquid fuels, use of natural gas vehicles, and the use of electric vehicles. For instance, China has begun to advance technology to convert coal to liquid fuels such as methanol and dimethyl ether, spurred in part by rising oil prices and energy security concerns. But these technologies are still a long way from being economical, and studies suggest they would produce even more carbon dioxide and other pollution than oil-based fuels do.[38] Natural gas supply, meanwhile, is very limited in China, although some cities like Beijing have made extensive use of natural gas buses in an attempt to reduce air pollution.

After several years of development, a number of Chinese automakers are planning to roll out both hybrid gasoline-electric and electric-only vehicles by 2010.[39] The national power grid company is also developing a fleet of thousands of electric-only vehicles for its own operations and plans to create networks of charging stations starting with the Beijing 2008 Olympics and the Shanghai 2010 World Expo.[40] Shanghai plans to have a fleet of electric buses in time for the Expo, possibly using "super-capacitor" storage rather than conventional batteries. Electric bicycles and scooters are already a huge and growing phenomenon throughout China, with many models now on the roads. This emerging trend toward electric vehicles may begin to compete with biofuels as an alternative means to improve energy security.

Sorghum crops.
© TataTimbo at Flickr.com.

China's Renewable Energy Future

In September 2007, Chen Deming, vice chairman of China's National Development and Reform Commission (NDRC), announced the government's finalized plan to accelerate the development of renewable energy in China, indicating that the country would invest 2 trillion yuan ($265 billion) in renewables, most of it from private sources.[1] The plan represents another clear step in the steady ratcheting up of China's renewable energy goals and commitments. The early successes of China's initial wave of renewables policies, starting in the 1990s, and its growing manufacturing base in the sector, are giving government and private leaders added confidence and ambition.

China is well positioned to develop renewable energy on an unprecedented scale in the years immediately ahead. It has already become the first developing country to promulgate such a comprehensive and strong set of national policies to promote renewables, and it is now positioned to "leapfrog" its renewable energy development ahead of industrial countries as well. China's status as the global leader in low-cost manufacturing may allow it to overcome the largest single hurdle to large-scale development of renewable energy worldwide: the ability to compete economically with fossil fuels.

In many other sectors, for technology after technology, China has achieved manufacturing costs that were once considered impossibly low. Achieving similar results in renewable energy will require continuing advances in policy, technical innovation, and human skills development, with a focus on stronger provincial and local policies as well as progress at the national level. Strong policies are needed to build technological capability, create new industries, and assemble the supporting institutions needed for sustained renewable energy development.

Much of China's progress in renewable energy to date has drawn on foreign technology. The next step is to develop indigenous technical skills and institutions to support research and technology development, including the skills needed for equipment design and manufacturing (for example in wind turbine blade design) as well as system design, component manufacturing, testing and verification, site selection, resource surveys, project planning and design, construction supervision, performance monitoring, repair and maintenance, and operations management. The NDRC has estimated that more than 100,000 skilled scientists and engineers will be needed by 2020, a tremendous increase from just several hundred such personnel employed today.[2]

China will need to develop a specialized energy technology research and development institution, perhaps along the lines of the U.S. National Renewable Energy Laboratory. Such an organization could conduct leading-edge research in support of Chinese industry; train engineers and scientists in design, manufacturing, testing, and management; and allow China to more closely follow international technology trends.

A national renewable energy research organization could also help fill an important gap in China: the lack of solid geographic resource assessments, especially compared to industrialized countries. Detailed resource maps are essential for project planning and financing and for minimizing investment risks. Although the Chinese Meteorological Research Institute has produced national resource assessments based on data collected at over 2,000 meteorological stations, such assessments are not adequate for detailed project planning and siting. And virtually no data exist on offshore wind resources, which offer great promise for future development. Skills and institutions for equipment certification and quality testing also need further strengthening.

The NDRC has begun developing national industry and research "roadmaps" that point the way to expansion and innovation, and these should be solidified and followed. Incentives and mechanisms for international technology cooperation among private firms are some of the keys to technology development. Building international partnerships, such as the Asia-Pacific Partnership to address climate change, can also help, along with financing tools like the Clean Development Mechanism (CDM) and carbon credits.

Renewable energy pricing and financial support are essential for the development of a sustained commercial industry in China—as other countries have discovered. Even with the 2005 Renewable Energy Law, wind power prices in China have been significantly lower than those found in other countries with robust wind markets, inhibiting the rate of development. Wind power concession bid-prices have been in the range of 0.4–0.5 RMB (5–6 U.S. cents) per kilowatt-hour. These are lower than prices found in the United States and Europe, which are typically in the range 6.5–8 cents per kilowatt-hour if subsidies are included.[3] Despite the relatively low prices, there has been ample availability of equity and debt capital for the sector. But financial conditions could change, and the government will need to be alert to the availability of capital for the sector. Concessionary financing may become more necessary for critical tasks such as pre-project planning.

China is a large country, and further development of renewable energy policies at the provincial and local levels is essential. There are many examples of local governments supporting renewables, with solar hot water heating and other technologies in Rizhao and the Baoding New High-Tech Industrial Development Zone being prominent examples.[4] (See Sidebar 7.) The city of Beijing is now also developing its own renewable energy strategy. At the provincial level, international initiatives such as the World Bank/Global Environment Facility China Renewable Energy Scale-Up Program (CRESP) are providing assistance to governments to pilot new policies in support of national objectives. And other bilateral and multilateral assistance agencies, such as the Asian Development Bank, United Nations Development Programme, and German Agency for Technical Cooperation (GTZ), are

Sidebar 7. Baoding New High-Tech Industrial Development Zone

The Baoding New High-Tech Industrial Development Zone embodies a new approach to technology development in China. Located close to Beijing, it was established in 1992 during a national frenzy of building high-tech zones to attract foreign investment. Since then, it has defined itself as a center of new energy technology and has won the title of "National New Energy and Energy Equipment Industrial Base."

Baoding now includes a solar PV industrial park and a wind power industrial park. Two large renewable energy manufacturers call Baoding home: Yingli Solar, one of China's top producers, and Zhonghang Baoding Huiteng Wind Energy, the country's leading wind-turbine blade manufacturer. The success stories of those two companies illustrate how local government support for renewable energy has enabled innovation.

The local government has made direct investments in many of Baoding's companies, helped them obtain outside financing and business partners, and has made connections with research institutes within China and abroad. Enticed by the existing industrial base, more new-energy enterprises have joined the zone in recent years, including manufacturers of solar PV and wind turbines, blades, control systems, and towers.

The marriage between the local government and enterprises is indispensable, as local enterprises and the business environment are far from mature, according to Ma Xuelu, head of the Baoding zone government. In his view, the most important benefit that this marriage brings is bypassing the red tape of the government "command role," which has hindered the pace of business development in the past.

Source: See Endnote 4 for this section.

helping at both the national and local levels.[5] Technology demonstrations, business-model testing, and market-building assistance have played a key role in China's current renewable energy momentum.

China will likely achieve its target of obtaining 15 percent of its energy from renewables by 2020, and may well exceed this goal. According to a number of scenarios, if China's commitment continues to grow, it could derive over 30 percent of its energy from renewables by 2050.[6] (See Sidebar 8.) This is consistent with recent global scenarios that suggest that the world could obtain 30–50 percent of its energy sup-

Sidebar 8. Future Scenarios for Renewable Energy in China

Several scenarios show renewable energy achieving significant shares in China by 2020 and 2050:

- A 2002 study by the China Energy Research Institute and the Lawrence Berkeley Laboratory considered three scenarios to 2020, all with the same GDP growth but differing in urbanization rates, technology development, and policies for energy supply and efficiency. A "promoting sustainability" scenario shows environmental policies and goals being met, while a "green-growth" scenario represents extra effort in energy efficiency and renewables. With green growth, the study envisioned renewables expanding to 200 gigawatts (GW) of large hydro, 30 GW of wind power, and 40 GW of small hydro, comparable to policy targets now in place.
- The Chinese Task Force on Energy Strategies and Technologies developed an "advanced technology" scenario that relies heavily on coal gasification, which expands from zero in 2000 to 60 percent of primary energy by 2050 (with coal falling to just 8 percent). At the same time, the primary energy share of renewables increases from 7 percent to 18 percent. Because of energy-intensity improvements, while the economy expands 13-fold by 2050, primary energy increases only 3.5-fold, from 42 exajoules (EJ) in 2000 to 135 EJ in 2050, accompanied by a ninefold increase in renewables from 2.8 EJ to 24 EJ.
- The World Business Council for Sustainable Development envisioned 38 percent of China's electricity from renewables by 2050, with a total of 1,000 GW of wind capacity.
- A Tsinghua University scenario shows the share of primary energy from renewables reaching 28 percent by 2050, with economy and energy projections to 2050 updated from the Chinese Task Force scenario. Although energy use increases 3.5-fold in China, primary energy share increases fourfold, leading to a 14-fold increase in renewables by 2050.

Source: See Endnote 6 for this section.

ply from renewables by 2050.[7] European scenarios have shown that up to 50 percent of primary energy from renewables would be possible as early as 2030 in Europe, and such a level for China is not implausible in the longer term.

China's total power generation from renewables could reach 400 gigawatts (GW) by 2020, nearly triple the 135 GW in place in 2006, with hydropower, wind, and solar photovoltaics (PV) making the most important contributions.[8] By 2050, this renewable power capacity might reach 2,000 or even 3,000 GW. This would yield avoided carbon dioxide emissions of 3.5–5 billion tons, equivalent to China's total emissions of the gas in 2005.[9] Specific technology prognoses are:

Wind power. Many believe the government's target of 30 GW of wind power by 2020 will be exceeded, perhaps reaching 60 GW. Beyond that, wind power could reach 100–200 GW by 2030 and as much as 600 GW by 2050.[10]

Solar PV. Estimates for the future of solar PV vary widely, but 2–10 GW by 2020 is not an unreasonable goal if expected cost reductions in technology occur in the coming years. Beyond that, 20–40 GW could be installed by 2030, and 500–1,000 GW by 2050.[11] By comparison, global grid-tied solar PV reached 5 GW in 2006, and some scenarios show as much as 500–1,000 GW of grid-tied solar PV worldwide by 2030.[12]

Solar thermal power. The future of concentrating solar thermal power generation is still uncertain. It is currently experiencing a renaissance in the United States and Europe, but has virtually no technology or commercial base in China. China has extensive desert areas that are well suited to solar thermal power generation, so if the technology becomes successful internationally and costs fall, it is possible that hundreds of GW of solar thermal power plants could be installed in China in the coming decades.[13]

Hydropower. China's hydropower capacity may reach 300–350 GW by 2020, before beginning to stabilize.[14]

Biomass power. It is unlikely that biomass power will make a major contribution beyond the government's target of 30 GW by 2020, as the resource is limited and collection of widely dispersed agricultural waste for use in large centralized generating plants is problematic in many areas if transport costs and logistics are considered. Given that there are only a few such plants yet running, the prospects of achieving even 30 GW by 2020 are uncertain.

Other. Smaller contributions from geothermal and tidal power of roughly 50 MW each are expected by 2020.

Achieving these goals in the power sector will depend on a number of factors. For wind power, these include the speed of domestic industry development and technology cost reductions, the evolution of government policy (including renewable portfolio requirements for the national generating companies), renewable power pricing levels, and the prospect for offshore wind. For biomass power, key factors include the viability of large-scale biomass power plants, the potential for developing industrial-scale biogas technology, the continuation of feed-in tariffs for favorable power pricing, and new technology development such as biomass gasifiers.

For solar PV, key factors include the speed of technology cost reductions, new policies to support building-integrated photovoltaics (BIPV) and other grid-tied applications (including feed-in prices or other incentives and construction standards and policies), and the speed with which electric power utilities accommodate so-called "distributed generation." Chinese utilities are not generally obligated to purchase power generated locally by their customers, nor are they as familiar with the engineering and institutional means for doing so.*

Prospects for continuing growth in solar hot water and heating use are good.[15] It is likely that more than one-third of China's households will be using solar hot water in the 2020–30 timeframe if current targets and policies are continued. Continued growth depends on additional policies and incentives for solar

---

* All forms of power generation could potentially be boosted by green power sales, in which consumers can choose to buy renewable power from suppliers offering it. Such sales (and also "utility green pricing") have become common in the United States and Europe where power sector restructuring has allowed retail competition. But retail competition does not yet exist in China.

Turbines at Dabancheng Wind Farm, Xinjiang. Some of China's best wind resources are made possible by the natural breach in Tian Mountain.

© Greenpeace/Hu Wei. Photo courtesy of Li Junfeng.

hot water and space heating, particularly integration into building codes and standards and construction practices. Other important needs are tax and export incentives, quality standards and labeling, and better consumer information. This is a challenge not just for the national government, but for municipal and provincial governments as well. The potential for export-led growth of the solar hot water manufacturing industry is large but remains untapped. Chinese manufacturers will need to understand and adapt to foreign technical standards and quality expectations, but the prize is a global market for low-cost Chinese solar hot water heaters.

Future prospects for biofuels depend on oil prices, technology development, and large-scale viability of plantation crops, although plantation crops may prove too expensive. Biofuels prospects may also depend on progress with electric vehicles and other substitutes for oil-based transportation. Prospects for cellulose-to-ethanol depend on technology commercialization and biorefinery sizes that are both efficient and suitable for the diffuse nature of China's rural biomass resources.

Prospects for rural use of renewable energy are diminishing as virtually all of China's rural population becomes electrified in the next 5–7 years. Nevertheless, biogas for cooking fuels will continue to be important, with expectations that the number of rural households using biogas will double by 2020. Markets for household solar electric and wind systems will continue to be important in more remote areas, particularly in western China. Prospects for village-scale power systems based on

renewables, following the completed 2004–06 Township Electrification Program, will depend on future government policy directions.

China is on track to assume global leadership in renewable energy in the years immediately ahead. Reaching this milestone in such a short time would constitute a remarkable achievement, with clear benefits for meeting China's energy needs and improving its energy security, while also reducing air pollution and lowering carbon emissions. China's leadership in renewable energy will provide a strong example for other developing countries, while helping to drive down renewable energy costs to the point that they become competitive with fossil fuels in rich and poor countries alike.

With fortunes to be made and men like Suntech's Shi Zhengrong leading the way, China's success in renewable energy seems all but assured. That success could constitute a true "tipping point" for the global energy economy, with far-reaching benefits not only for 1.3 billion Chinese, but also for the world's 5 billion other people.

Endnotes

China's Energy Crossroads

1. Shi was worth an estimated $2.2 billion in 2006, per "#350 Zhengrong Shi," in "World's Richest People," *Forbes Magazine*, www.forbes.com/lists/2006/10/EP46.html.

2. Suntech produced 158 megawatts (MW) in 2006, behind Sharp of Japan (434 MW), Kyocera of Japan (180 MW), and Q-cells of Germany (253 MW), per *PV News*, April 2007.

3. Joe McDonald, "China's 'Sun King' Hails Clean Energy," *Associated Press*, 22 April 2007; KPMG Huazhen, "Alternative Energies in China: Which Way Will the Wind Blow?" (Beijing: 2007), p. 7.

4. Renewable Energy Policy Network for the 21st Century (REN21), *Renewables 2007 Global Status Report* (Paris: REN21 and Washington, DC: Worldwatch Institute, forthcoming). See also REN 21, *Renewables 2005 Global Status Report* and REN21, *Renewables Global Status Report 2006 Update*; and Janet Sawin, *Mainstreaming Renewable Energy in the 21st Century*, Worldwatch Paper 169 (Washington, DC: Worldwatch Institute, 2004).

5. Figure 1 from the following sources: data for 1990––2004 from Energy Bureau of National Development and Reform Commission (NDRC) and National Bureau of Statistics of China (NBS), Department of Industry and Transport Statistics, *China Energy Statistical Yearbook 2005* (Beijing: China Statistics Press, 2006); 2005 data from NDRC, *Eleventh Five-Year Energy Plan* (Beijing: April 2007); 2006 data from Chen Deiming, keynote speech at the National Solar Thermal Energy Conference, Jinan, China, April 2007. Similar figures for 2005 and 2006 are included in BP, *Statistical Review of World Energy 2007* (London: 2007).

6. World Bank, *World Development Indicators 2007* (Washington, DC: 2007), with most recent data for 2004, which gives China as 1.2 tons of energy equivalent (toe) per capita. Figure for 2006 recalculated as 1.3 toe/capita, using a population estimate for 2006 of 1.31 billion, per Chen, op. cit. note 5.

7. Estimates of rural versus urban energy use are difficult to find; estimate of three times more electricity and commercial energy comes from household surveys by the NBS, but does not account for rural biomass and biogas use, which represent a substantial share of total energy consumption for many rural households. Urban population estimates from "China's Urban Population Grows to 376 Million," *People's Daily*, 17 August 2000, and from NBS, *Report on Economic and Social Development Between the 16th and 17th National Congress* (Beijing: 26 September 2007).

8. BP, op. cit. note 5.

9. Electricity consumption in 2006 was 2,834 terrawatt-hours (TWh), of which 80 percent was coal fired, per China Electricity Council, (CEC) *Annual Report* (Beijing: 2007).

10. Electricity consumption in 2000 was 1,347 TWh, per Energy Bureau of NDRC and NBS, Department of Industry and Transport Statistics, op. cit. note 5; electricity consumption in 2006 from CEC, op. cit. note 9.

11. CEC, op. cit. note 9; International Energy Agency, *Electricity Information 2007* (Paris: 2007). In 2006, 90 gigawatts (GW) of coal was added in China.

12. Asia-Pacific Energy Research Center (APERC), "Energy in China: Transportation, Electric Power and Fuel Markets" (Tokyo: 2004).

13. EU figure is for EU-25. EU and U.S. figures from REN21, op. cit. note 4; China figure from CEC, op. cit. note 9.

14. Total hydropower capacity was 129 GW at the end of 2006, with 11.5 GW added hydropower during 2006, per Chinese Renewable Energy Industries Association (CREIA) and Energy Bureau of NDRC, *China Renewable Energy Outlook 2007* (Beijing: 2007).

15. Average residential electricity consumption per capita in 2004 (including both rural and urban households) was 190 kilowatt-hours (kWh), per Energy Bureau of NDRC and NBS, Department of Industry and Transport Statistics, op. cit. note 5. Assuming 3.2 people per urban household and accounting for the urban/rural difference in consumption and urban population (see note 7), and considering other published estimates of residential electricity consumption, typical annual urban electricity consumption of 1200–1600 kWh per household is reasonable (this is only one-fifth as much as a typical U.S. urban household). See for example, Debbie Brockett et al., "A Tale of Five Cities: The China Residential Energy Consumption Survey," in *ACEEE Summer Study on Building Energy Efficiency* (Berkeley, CA: Lawrence Berkeley National Laboratory, 2002). Three Gorges production from Government of China, "Advanced Technologies Used in the Three Gorges Project," 17 May 2006, at www.gov.cn.

Endnotes

16. The environmental and social impacts of large hydro projects tend to put them in a separate category from other renewable energy technologies. The Three Gorges project resulted in displacement of an estimated 2 million people. The new Xiangjiaba project is expected to lead to the relocation of 88,000 to 150,000 people and to submerge six counties, per "Concerns as New Dam to Displace Thousands." *South China Morning Post*, 27 November 2006.

17. One projection shows nuclear power capacity reaching 40 GW by 2020, per NDRC, "Mid and Long Term Development Plan (2005–2020) for Nuclear Power in China," initially approved by the State Council on 22 March 2006. See also "China's Nuclear Fuel Breaks the Allocation of Macro Planning; Uranium Won't Tie to Electricity Price Soon," *Shanghai Securities News*, 7 September 2007.

18. Jack Perkowski, "The Battle for China's Auto Market," presented at JPMorgan's "Hands-On China Series," Beijing, April 2007 (Hong Kong: JPMorgan, 2007).

19. Ibid.

20. "Global Vehicle Sales Growth Expected to Stall in 2007: Scotiabank," *CBC News*, 28 December 2006; U.S. Department of Energy, "Fact #474: Changes in Vehicles per Capita Around the World," 18 June 2007, at www1.eere.energy.gov/vehiclesandfuels/facts/2007_fcvt_fotw474.html.

21. Perkowski, op. cit. note 18.

22. BP, op. cit. note 5; William Mellor and Le-Min Lim, "China Drills Where Others Dare Not Seek Oil," *International Herald Tribune*, 2 October 2006; Suzanne C. Hunt and Janet L. Sawin with Peter Stair, "Cultivating Renewable Alternatives to Oil" in Worldwatch Institute, *State of the World 2006* (New York: W.W. Norton & Company, 2006), pp. 61–77.

23. BP, op. cit. note 5.

24. The International Energy Agency's *World Energy Outlook 2007* (Paris: 2007) projects Chinese production of 3.8 million barrels per day by 2015 and 3.4 million barrels per day by 2030.

25. World Bank and China State Environmental Protection Administration (SEPA), "Cost of Pollution in China: Economic Estimates of Physical Damages," working paper (Washington, DC: 1 February 2007).

26. Joseph Kahn and Jim Yardley, "As China Roars, Pollution Reaches Deadly Extremes," *New York Times*, 26 August 2007.

27. SEPA and NBS, *China Green National Accounting Study Report 2004* (Beijing: 7 September 2006).

28. Kahn and Yardley, op. cit. note 26. See also World Bank, "China: Air, Land, and Water; Environmental Priorities for a New Millennium" (Washington, DC: 2001) and World Bank, "Clear Water, Blue Skies: China's Environment in the New Century" (Washington, DC: 1997).

29. Elisabeth Economy, "The Great Leap Backward?" *Foreign Affairs*, September/October 2007.

30. U.S. Environmental Protection Agency estimates cited in Terence Chea, "Pollution from China Drifting East," *Associated Press*, 30 July 2006.

31. According to Dutch researchers, China's total carbon dioxide emissions exceeded U.S. emissions in 2007, per Netherlands Environmental Assessment Agency, "China Now No. 1 in CO2 Emissions; USA in Second Position" (Bilthoven: 19 June 2007). But the Chinese government has not agreed with the Dutch pronouncement and puts the transition closer to 2010.

32. World Bank, *World Development Indicators 2007* (Washington, DC: 2007), with energy statistics for 2004 and carbon statistics for 2003.

33. National Climate Change Coordination Group Office of China, "China National Climate Change Program" (Beijing: 2007).

34. See, for example, Wang Jun, "The Energy Situation, Policy and Development of Clean Coal Technology in China," *Energy for Sustainable Development* vol. 7, no. 4 (2003), pp. 15–17; Li Zheng et al., "Polygeneration Energy System Based on Coal Gasification," *Energy for Sustainable Development* vol. 7, no. 4 (2003), pp. 57–62; Peter Fairley, "China's Coal Future," *Technology Review*, January/February 2007. A few supercritical coal plants are already operating.

35. Figure 2 from Energy Bureau of NDRC and NBS, Department of Industry and Transport Statistics, op. cit. note 5.

36. For an historical treatment of past gains in energy intensity going back to the 1970s, see Jonathan E. Sinton and Mark D. Levine, "Energy Efficiency in China: Accomplishments and Challenges," *Energy Policy*, vol. 26, no. 11 (1998), pp. 813–29.

37. NDRC, "China Medium and Long-Term Energy Conservation Plan" (Beijing: 2005); KPMG Huazhen, op. cit. note 3.

38. NDRC, op. cit. note 37.

39. Ibid.

40. Ma Kai, Chairman, NDRC, reports delivered to the National People's Congress, March and July 2007; Shi Guosheng, "10 Priorities in Energy Saving and Pollution Reduction," *People's Daily*, 27 August 2007.

41. Ma, op. cit. note 40.

42. Ibid.

The Promise of Renewables

1. Renewables 2004 Web site, www.renewables2004.de.

2. In 2005, China hosted a follow-up conference to Renewables 2004, the Beijing International Renewable Energy Conference, at which officials reiterated the 16 percent target and announced that $180 billion would be invested in renewable energy through 2020. "China to Spend $180 Billion to Boost Renewable Energy Use," *Agence France Presse*, 7 November 2005; National Development and Reform Commission (NDRC), "Medium and Long-Term Development Plan for Renewable Energy in China" (Beijing: September 2007).

Endnotes

3. Renewable Energy Policy Network for the 21st Century (REN21), *Renewables 2007 Global Status Report* (Paris: REN21 and Washington, DC: Worldwatch Institute, forthcoming). Large hydropower investment in China was another $8–10 billion in 2006, bringing total renewables investment to about $17–20 billion that year.

4. Data in Table 1 are based on unpublished research by the Chinese Renewable Energy Industries Association (CREIA) and the China Energy Research Institute, supplemented by other sources, including Li Junfeng and Wang Sicheng, *China Solar PV Report 2007* (Beijing: China Environmental Science Press, 2007) and Shi Pengfei, "Wind Power in China," presentation in Guangzhou, China, 23 March 2007 (Beijing: China General Certification Center). Actual renewables numbers for 2006 include 480 terrawatt-hours (TWh) of hydropower, 10 TWh of biomass power, 3 TWh of wind power, and 15 million tons of coal equivalent of primary energy from solar hot water. Estimated renewables electricity for 2020 corresponds to the government's 2020 technology targets (see Table 2), including 820 TWh of large hydropower, 260 TWh of small hydropower, 69 TWh of wind power, 125 TWh of biomass power, and 2.2 TWh of solar PV. There is no government target for share of electricity generation, so the 2020 electricity share given here is an estimate, while the 15 percent primary energy share is an official target. Estimates for 2020 total energy and electricity from Tsinghua University, Institute of Energy and Environmental Economics. China's convention for counting the primary energy contribution from renewable electricity corresponds to the "IEA Method," which counts only the direct energy value of the electricity, as opposed to the "BP Method," which counts the equivalent primary energy needed to generate that amount of electricity. The share of primary energy from renewables will be more than two times higher than the figures shown in Table 1 if the BP Method is applied instead (roughly 18 percent in 2006 and 31 percent in 2020 using a BP-assumed power plant efficiency of 38 percent and considering the amounts of non-electricity renewables such as solar hot water and biofuels that are counted the same under both methods). For a full explanation of these two different accounting methods, see Eric Martinot et al., "Renewable Energy Futures: Targets, Scenarios, and Pathways," *Annual Review of Environment and Resources*, vol. 32 (2007), forthcoming.

5. American Council On Renewable Energy (ACORE), CREIA, European Renewable Energy Council (EREC), and World Council for Renewable Energy (WCRE), "Joint Assessment of Reaching 25% Renewable Energy by the Year 2025," memorandum of understanding signed at the Great Wall Renewable Energy Forum, Beijing, October 2006. See also "Compact Signed to Raise Renewable Energy to 25% of Global Energy Supply," RenewableEnergyAccess.com, 25 October 2006.

6. NDRC, op. cit. note 2; REN21, op. cit. note 3.

7. Table 2 from Ibid. Ethanol target for 2010 is for 2 million tons of added ethanol production from non-food-grain fuels. Solar PV targets include 50 megawatts (MW) of grid-tied PV by 2010 and 1 gigawatt (GW) of grid-tied PV by 2020.

8. Estimate of 1,000–1,200 GW from Zhang Xiliang and He Jiankun, "Strategies and Policies on Promoting Massive Renewable Energy Development," *Proceedings of China Renewable Energy Development Strategy Workshop, Beijing, 28 October 2005* (Beijing: Tsinghua University Institute of Nuclear and New Energy Technology and Tsinghua-BP Clean Energy Research and Education Center, 2005). Note that there is a difference between comparing share of capacity and share of electricity generation.

9. NDRC, op. cit. note 2.

10. "The Renewable Energy Law of the People's Republic of China," adopted at the 14th Session of the Standing Committee of the 10th National People's Congress, Beijing, China, 28 February 2005. For a critical analysis of the law, see Judith A. Cherni and Joanna Kentish, "Renewable Energy Policy and Electricity Market Reforms in China," *Energy Policy*, vol. 35 (2007), pp. 3616–29.

11. NDRC, "Measures for Pricing and Cost-Sharing Management" and "Management Guidelines" (Beijing: January 2006), both available at www.martinot.info/china.htm. Feed-in tariff for biomass applies to the first 30,000 hours of operation.

12. Azure International, "China Concession Wind Projects Update" (Beijing: 2006). Guangdong province also established a de-facto feed-in tariff regime, and other provinces are following suit. Most provincial policies apply only to projects less than 50 MW, although one Shanghai project was for a 100 MW offshore wind farm. These provincial-level (and even sub-provincial-level) regimes have become the primary form of private foreign project development for wind power. Sebastian Meyer, Azure International, personal communication with Eric Martinot, Beijing, 8 October 2007.

13. NDRC, op. cit. note 2.

14. Tax figures from various official documents of the China National Taxation Administration.

15. Ministry of Finance, "Renewable Energy Fund Interim Management Measures" (Beijing: 2006).

16. Xu Jing, speech at Beijing Renewable Energy Development Forum, Beijing, 12 January 2006.

17. REN21, op. cit. note 3. German investment in 2006 was about $11–12 billion.

18. REN21, op. cit. note 3; "NDRC to Make Solar Energy Application Compulsory," *Xinhua News Service*, 8 May 2007.

19. See sources for Tables 1 and 2, op. cit. notes 4 and 7.

20. CREIA and the Energy Bureau of NDRC, *China Renewable Energy Outlook 2007* (Beijing: 2007); REN21 op. cit. note 3.

21. Ibid. See also Wang Xiaohua and Li Jingfei, "Influence of Using Household Biogas Digesters on Household Energy Consumption in Rural Areas—A Case Study in Lianshui County in China," *Renewable and Sustainable Energy Reviews*, vol. 9, no. 2 (2005), pp. 229–36; Eric Martinot et al., "Renewable Energy Markets in Developing Countries," *Annual Review of Energy and the*

Environment, vol. 27 (2002), pp. 309–48; World Bank Energy Sector Management Assistance Project (ESMAP), *Energy for Rural Development in China: An Assessment Based on a Joint Chinese/ESMAP Study in Six Counties* (Washington, DC: 1996).

22. CREIA and Energy Bureau of NDRC, op. cit. note 20; REN21 op. cit. note 3.

23. CREIA and Energy Bureau of NDRC, op. cit. note 20.

24. Ibid.

25. In 2006, solar PV cell production reached 370 MW in China, 927 MW in Japan, 510 MW in Germany, and 200 MW in the United States, per *PV News*, April 2007.

26. REN21 op. cit. note 3.

Wind Power

1. Shi Pengfei, "Wind Power in China," presentation, Guangzhou, China, 23 March 2007; Shi Pengfei, "2006 Wind Installations in China" (Beijing: China General Certification Center, 2007).

2. Renewable Energy Policy Network for the 21st Century (REN21), *Renewables 2007 Global Status Report* (Paris: REN21 and Washington, DC: Worldwatch Institute, forthcoming).

3. Azure International, "China Concession Wind Projects Update" (Beijing: 2006). At least 1 gigawatt (GW) was reported installed during the first six months of 2007, per Sebastian Meyer, Azure International, personal communication with Eric Martinot, Beijing, 8 October 2007.

4. Ibid. The 8 GW includes de-facto "policy orders" through 2010.

5. Sebastian Meyer, "Wind Project Finance in China: A Quick Snap-Shot," presentation at Renewable Energy Finance Forum, Beijing, 29–30 March 2007.

6. Sidebar 1 from the following sources: Shi, op. cit. note 1; Meyer, op. cit. note 5; Azure International, op. cit. note 3. Other concession-award weightings besides price in 2006 were for turbine localization (35 percent), technical proposal (20 percent), financing proposal and ability (10 percent), and project financing (10 percent). Preferential tariffs awarded during the process of concession bidding apply to the first 3 billion kilowatt-hours (kWh) of electricity production, which for a 100 MW facility could be 12–15 years. After that, non-concessional local grid tariffs apply. Bidding on a further 9 projects was initiated by the government in late 2007, with a total capacity of 1,100 MW. For a critical review of wind energy policy, see Adrian Lema and Kristian Ruby, "Between Fragmented Authoritarianism and Policy Coordination: Creating a Chinese Market for Wind Energy," Energy Policy, vol. 35 (2007), pp. 3879–90, and Jean Ku et al., "The Future Is Now: Accelerating Wind Development in China," *Renewable Energy World*, July/August 2005.

7. China wind resource maps from the China Meteorology Research Institute, Beijing.

8. Shi, op. cit. note 1.

9. Ibid.

10. United Nations Environment Programme, Solar and Wind Energy Resource Assessment Project, "China Wind Energy Resource Assessment" (Paris: 2006), at http://swera.unep.net.

11. In 2006, 55 percent of China's added wind turbines came from foreign manufacturers, although most of these were actually produced in Chinese subsidiaries of the foreign companies; 41 percent came from Chinese manufacturers, and 4 percent from joint ventures. Cumulative market share as of 2006 was 66 percent foreign, 31 percent domestic, and 3 percent joint ventures. See Shi, op. cit. note 1.

12. Sidebar 2 from the following sources: World Wind Energy Association, "World Wind Energy Award 2006 Goes to Chinese Wind Turbine Manufacturer Goldwind and Wu Gang," press release (Bonn: 6 November 2006); Shi, op. cit. note 1; Yingling Liu, "Made in China, Or Made by China? Chinese Wind Turbine Manufacturers Struggle to Enter Own Market," *China Watch* (Worldwatch Institute), 19 May 2006; "Wu Gang: Who Competes for 'Wind'?!" *China Business News*, 25 October 2006; Ruan Xiaoqin, "Overseas IPO by Goldwind Thwarted," *Shanghai Security News*, 24 August 2006; Xu Jianjun, "Goldwind Went IPO on A Share Before Considering an Overseas IPO," *China Securities News*, 3 April 2007.

13. Shi, op. cit. note 1.

14. Ibid.

15. Ibid.

16. Ibid.

17. Ibid.

18. Ibid.

Solar Power

1. United Nations Environment Programme, Solar and Wind Energy Resource Assessment Project, "China Wind Energy Resource Assessment" (Paris: 2006), at http://swera.unep.net.

2. Global capacity from Renewable Energy Policy Network for the 21st Century (REN21), *Renewables 2007 Global Status Report* (Paris: REN21 and Washington, DC: Worldwatch Institute, forthcoming). Chinese Renewable Energy Industries Association (CREIA) and the Energy Bureau of the National Development and Reform Commission (NDRC), *China Renewable Energy Outlook 2007* (Beijing: 2007); Wang Sicheng, "Current Status of PV in China," presentation at the Great Wall Renewable Energy Forum, Beijing, 23–27 October 2006; Zhao Yumen, Wu Dacheng, and Li Xudong, "The Status of Photovoltaic Industry and Market Development in China," prepared for the Great Wall Renewable Energy Forum, Beijing, 24–26 October 2006 (Beijing: Beijing Solar Energy Institute, 2006); Wang Sicheng, "Present Situation and Prediction on Photovoltaics in China," in *Proceedings of China Renewable Energy Development Strategy Workshop, Beijing, 28 October 2005* (Beijing: Tsinghua University Institute of Nuclear and New Energy Technology and Tsinghua-BP Clean Energy Research and Education Center, 2005). All documents available at

www.martinot.info/china.htm.

3. Sidebar 3 from the following sources: W.L. Wallace, H.O. Wu, and Z.Y. Wang, "Experience for Sustainable Development of Rural Energy in China," paper prepared for the Great Wall Renewable Energy Forum, Beijing, 23–27 October 2006 (Beijing: Project office of UNDP/GEF Capacity Building for the Rapid Commercialization of Renewable Energy), available at www.martinot.info/china.htm; Ma Shenghong, "China 'Brightness' and 'Township Electrification' programs," presentation at Renewables 2004 conference, Bonn, Germany, June 2004; Jean Ku, Debra Lew, and Ma Shenghong, "Sending Electricity to Townships," *Renewable Energy World*, September/October 2003, pp. 56–67; John Byrne, Bo Shen, and William Wallace, "The Economics of Sustainable Energy for Rural Development: A Study of Renewable Energy in Rural China," *Energy Policy*, vol. 26, no. 1 (1998), pp. 45–54; CREIA estimates and other unpublished information.

4. CREIA and Energy Bureau of NDRC, op. cit. note 2; Wang, op. cit. note 2; Zhao, Wu, and Li, op. cit. note 2.

5. Ibid.

6. Ibid.

7. REN21, op. cit. note 2.

8. Yingling Liu, "Shanghai Embarks on 100,000 Solar Roofs Initiative," *China Watch* (Worldwatch Institute), 10 November 2005.

9. Wang Jun, "Light the Green Torch," *Beijing Review*, 22 March 2007; Wang Fengling, Secretary-General, Jiangsu Province Renewable Energy Association, Nanjing, personal communication with Eric Martinot, November 2006.

10. Wang Jun, op. cit. note 9.

11. "Energy-Saving Projects Initiated for Olympics," *Xinhua News Agency*, 6 July 2006; "Light the Green Torch," *Beijing Review*, 22 March 2007.

12. Companies include Tianwei Yingli, LDK Solar, China Solar Energy, Nanjing PV Tech, Trina, Solarfun, Suntech, Canadian Solar, and ReneSola, per "Chinese PV Manufacturers: The Race to IPO," *New Energy Finance* (London), 30 January 2007.

13. CREIA and Energy Bureau of NDRC, op. cit. note 2; Wang, op. cit. note 2; Zhao, Wu, and Li, op. cit. note 2.

14. Table 3 from Ibid.

15. Actual solar PV production in 2006 and 2007 is significantly less than the production capacity numbers given, as capacity numbers reflect year-end situation only. Actual production in 2006 was 370 megawatts (MW), per *PV News*, April 2007. Projected 2007 year-end manufacturing capacity includes Suntech (470 MW), China Sunergy (160 MW), Baoding Yingli (200 MW), JA Solar (175 MW), Solarfun (240 MW), Shenzhen Topray (22.5 MW), and others (228 MW). Suntech is expected to be third worldwide in 2007, behind Sharp and Q-Cells, per *PV News*, September 2007, p. 8. Suntech now plans to have 850 MW of capacity in place by end of 2010, per Sascha Rentzing, "Sun Aplenty," *New Energy*, June 2007, p. 50.

16. Sidebar 4 from the following sources: Li Peng, "2007, New Ray of Hope for New Energy," *China Economic Times*, 17 January 2007; Chen Wei, "Solar PV Giant Suntech Favored Shanghai Market," *Wen Hui Po*, 11 September 2006; Wang You, "Threats behind the Starry Development of the Solar Industry," *China Business News*, 25 April 2007; Joe Mcdonald, "Chinese Scientist Cashes in on 'Clean Energy,'" *Associated Press*, 23 April 2007; Chang Huiying, "Suntech's New R&D and Manufacture Center Set Up in Shanghai, " *China News Service Shanghai*, 21 August 2006; Huang Jie, "Suntech CEO Shi Zhengrong: China's Next Richest Man," *National Business Daily*, 4 January 2006; Shen Weiyan and Gao Jie, "Suntech Running after the Sun," *China Environmental News*, 26 April 2006; Zhao Jianfei, "Renewable Energy Warming Up," *Caijing Magazine*, 14 May 2007; "Forbes to Name Richest Person in Chinese Mainland," *Xinhua News Agency*, 11 October 2006; Ruan Xiaoqin, "Suntech Net Revenue Jumped 165% in 2006," *Shanghai Securities News*, 15 March 2007; "Suntech Starts Construction of Shanghai Thin Film Plant," RenewableEnergyAccess.com, 24 May 2007; Suntech Web site, www.suntech-power.com.

17. Wang, "Current Status of PV in China," op. cit. note 2.

18. Ibid.

19. Ibid; Zhao, Wu, and Li, op. cit. note 2.

20. Zhao, Wu, and Li, op. cit. note 2.

21. Ibid; Wang, "Present Situation and Prediction on Photovoltaics in China," op. cit. note 2; CREIA estimates.

22. Wang, "Current Status of PV in China," op. cit. note 2; Zhao, Wu, and Li, op. cit. note 2.

23. Zhao, Wu, and Li, op. cit. note 2.

Solar Hot Water and Heating

1. Chinese Renewable Energy Industries Association (CREIA) and the Energy Bureau of the National Development and Reform Commission (NDRC), *China Renewable Energy Outlook 2007* (Beijing: 2007); Shi Lishan and others, "China's Solar Thermal Industry Review" (Beijing: NDRC, 2005, unpublished); Luo Zhentao, "The Present Condition and Forecast Prediction of Solar Energy-Thermal Utilization in China," in *Proceedings of China Renewable Energy Development Strategy Workshop, Beijing, 28 October 2005* (Beijing: Tsinghua University Institute of Nuclear and New Energy Technology and Tsinghua-BP Clean Energy Research and Education Center, 2005); Luo Zhentao, "Development and Prospects of Solar Water Heating," in *Annual Report on China's New Energy Industry* (Beijing: China New Energy Chamber of Commerce, 2006). Including unglazed collectors for swimming pools, which REN21 and others consider to be a separate application, the global total in 2006 was about 152 million square meters, per REN21 Renewable Energy Policy Network for the 21st Century (REN21), *Renewables 2007 Global Status Report* (Paris: REN21 and Washington, DC: Worldwatch Institute, forthcoming).

2. CREIA and Energy Bureau of NDRC, op. cit. note 1.

3. Werner Weiss, Irene Bergmann, and Gerhard

Endnotes

Faninger, "Solar Heat Worldwide: Markets and Contribution to the Energy Supply 2005," prepared for the Solar Heating and Cooling Programme, International Energy Agency (Paris: April 2007), p. 17.

4. James R. Areddy, "Heat for the Tubs of China," *Wall Street Journal*, 31 March 2006.

5. Sidebar 5 from the following sources: Li Zhaoqian, presentation at World Urban Forum III, Vancouver, Canada, 19–23 June 2006; Wang Shuguang, e-mails and discussions with Xuemei Bai, Commonwealth Scientific and Industrial Research Organization (CSIRO), Campbell, Australia, August and October 2006; Rizhao City Government, *2005 Rizhao Economic and Social Development Statistic Bulletin*, available at www.rizhao.gov.cn, viewed 10 June 2006; Rizhao City Construction Committee, internal statistics; Fao Yanhui, Office of the Mayor of Rizhao, e-mail to Janet Sawin, Worldwatch Institute, 22 February 2007; Li Zhaoqian, discussion with Xuemei Bai, 17 June 2006; State Environmental Protection Agency, *2005 Annual Report of Urban Environmental Management and Comprehensive Pollution Control* (Beijing: 2006); "More than 300 Peking University Professors Bought Houses in Rizhao," *Beijing Youth Daily*, 11 August 2006. Energy savings calculation based on 560,000 square meters installed, reportedly displacing 348 gigawatt-hours (GWh) of electricity (or equivalent) each year. The same answer results by considering China's overall solar hot water usage, 15 million tons of coal equivalent of primary energy saved from 80 million square meters installed in 2006, or the energy equivalent of the coal required to generate 348 GWh (at 3.2 kilowatt-hours produced per kilogram of coal).

6. CREIA estimates.

7. Luo, "Development and Prospects of Solar Water Heating," op. cit. note 1.

8. Li Hua, "From Quantity to Quality: How China's Solar Thermal Industry Will Need to Face up to Market Challenges," *Renewable Energy World*, vol. 8, no. 1 (2005).

9. Ibid.

10. CREIA estimates.

11. In contrast to other markets, China's market is dominated by glass vacuum tube solar water heaters, with a market share of 88 percent in 2003. Ten brands of solar water heaters had annual sale volumes of over 100 million RMB, including Anhui Liguang, Lianyungang Taiyangyu Company, Nantong Sangxia Company, Guangdong Jiaputong Company, Yunnan Tongle Company, and Shandong Sangle Company. But the market is still highly diverse, as those top-ten brands had a combined market share of only 20 percent. Luo, "Development and Prospects of Solar Water Heating," op. cit. note 1.

12. "NDRC to Make Solar Energy Application Compulsory," *Xinhua News Agency*, 8 May 2007.

13. "Cloudy Outlook for China's Solar Industry," *Agence France Presse*, 9 February 2007.

14. NDRC, "China's Long and Middle-Term Renewable Energy Plan" (Beijing: 2007), announced and summarized by *Xinhua News Agency*, 4 September 2007.

15. CREIA estimates.

16. Ibid.

17. Chinese exports could prove a boon for solar hot water consumers around the world, but likely at the expense of European producers. See Li Hua, "China's Solar Thermal Industry: Threat or Opportunity for European Companies?" *Renewable Energy World*, July/August 2002.

18. Luo, "Development and Prospects of Solar Water Heating," op. cit. note 1.

19. Huang Ming, personal communication with Eric Martinot, September 2007.

20. Ibid.

21. W.L. Wallace, S.J. Liu, and Z.Y. Wang, "Development of a Standards, Testing, and Certification Program to Support the Domestic Solar Water Heating Market in China," prepared for the Great Wall Renewable Energy Forum, Beijing, 23–27 October 2006 (Beijing: Project office of UNDP/GEF Capacity Building for the Rapid Commercialization of Renewable Energy).

Biomass Power and Biofuels

1. Chinese Renewable Energy Industries Association (CREIA) and the Energy Bureau of the National Development and Reform Commission (NDRC), *China Renewable Energy Outlook 2007* (Beijing: 2007).

2. Biomass gasification for power generation is a third less significant but potentially important form of renewable power generation. Much research has been done in the last several decades on small-scale biomass gasification in China, including fixed bed and circulating fluidized bed (CFB) gasifiers. So far, only rice-husk gasification is relatively mature, per C.Z. Wu et al., "An Economic Analysis of Biomass Gasification and Power Generation in China," *Bioresource Technology*, vol. 83 (2002), pp. 65–70. CFB gasifiers are typically 400–2,000 kilowatts (kW) in size, with efficiency of 65–75 percent; down-draft gasifiers are typically 60–200 kW in size with efficiency of 75 percent. Estimates of the number of small-scale (160–200 kW) gasification projects for power generation vary, but probably number in the hundreds, per Wu, op. cit. this note, and M. Xiao, "Development of Biomass Converstion Technology and Industry in China – CAREI Annual Report 2002," International Conference on Bioenergy Utilization and Environment Protection, 6th LAMNET Workshop, Dalian, China, 24–26 September 2003. In past years, a few larger demonstration projects of 1 megawatt (MW) and larger have been conducted. A few hundred biomass gasification projects exist in rural areas to produce gas for household heating and cooking via small local networks rather than for power generation.

3. W.L. Wallace, H.O. Wu, and Z.Y. Wang, "Boosting the Market for the Commercialization of Industrial Scale Biogas Projects in China," presented at the Great Wall Renewable Energy Forum, Beijing, 24–26 October 2006. Biogas from recycling animal wastes in large-scale livestock farms only partly addresses the environmental issues associated with such farms; see Danielle Nierenberg, *Happier Meals: Rethinking the Global Meat*

Endnotes

Industry, Worldwatch Paper 171 (Washington, DC: Worldwatch Institute, 2005).

4. Ibid. Another estimate gives 100 billion cubic meters of potential biogas production as early as 2010. See J. Li et al., "Assessment of Sustainable Energy Potential of Non-Plantation Biomass Resources in China," *Biomass and Bioenergy*, vol. 29 (2005), pp. 167–77.

5. Wallace, Wu, and Wang, op. cit. note 3.

6. Sidebar 6 from the following sources: biogas from CREIA and Energy Bureau of NDRC, op. cit. note 1; from Wang Xiaohua and Li Jingfei, "Influence of Using Household Biogas Digesters on Household Energy Consumption in Rural Areas—A Case Study in Lianshui County in China," *Renewable and Sustainable Energy Reviews*, vol. 9, no. 2 (2005), pp. 229–36; and from Gu Shuhua, "Biogas Resources of China and Its Exploitation and Utilization, in *Proceedings of China Renewable Energy Development Strategy Workshop, Beijing, 28 October 2005* (Beijing: Tsinghua University Institute of Nuclear and New Energy Technology and Tsinghua-BP Clean Energy Research and Education Center, 2005). Pellets from X. Zeng, Y. Ma, and L. Ma, "Utilization of Straw in Biomass Energy in China," *Renewable and Sustainable Energy Review*, vol. 11 (2007), pp. 976–87 and from A.P.C. Faaij, "Bio-Energy in Europe: Changing Technology Choices," *Energy Policy*, vol. 34 (2006), pp. 322–42.

7. Ma Longlong, "The Expectation of Biomass Power Development in China," in *Proceedings of China Renewable Energy Development Strategy Workshop, Beijing, 28 October 2005*, op. cit. note 6.

8. "China's First Biomass Power Plant Goes into Operation," *Xinhua News Agency*, 1 December 2006.

9. National Bio-Energy Company, "The Ceremony of the Successful Opening of the First State-Designated Biomass-Power Generating Demonstration Project," 11 December 2006, at www.nbe.cn/news_english.asp?newsid=284.

10. Competing uses for crop residues include returning to the field as fertilizer, using as animal fodder, and industrial uses such as papermaking; thus, only a fraction of total residues will be available for energy.   Most studies estimate about 15–20 percent of crop residues are used for fertilizer, 2–3 percent for papermaking, 25–35 percent for fodder, and the rest available for energy. Li et al., op. cit. note 4; Zeng, Ma, and Ma, op. cit. note 6; China Ministry of Agriculture (MOA) and U.S. Department of Energy (DOE) Expert Team, "Assessment of Biomass Resource Availability in China (Beijing: China Environmental Science Press, 1998). Estimates for the total quantity of crop residues and the amount available for energy vary. One study estimates that from 1997–2010, about 370–390 million tons of residues per year will be available for energy, per Li et al., op. cit. note 4. Another puts residues available for energy from 1995–2010 at an approximately constant 360–380 million tons per year, per MOA/DOE Project Expert Team, op. cit. this note. Both studies take into account estimated trends for crop production and changes in crop residue utilization for industry and animal husbandry. One upper bound on crop residues for energy through 2050 is given

as 470 million tons, per E.D. Larson et al., "Future Implications of China's Energy-Technology Choices," *Energy Policy*, vol. 31 (2003), pp. 1189–1204.

11. In source material, it is difficult to determine which papers include wood waste from industrial processes as part of the forestry waste resource, leading to a wider variation in estimates. One study estimates total forest biomass resources (as of the late 1990s) at 227 million tons, of which 104 million tons would be available for energy. Another study estimates 120 million tons available for energy. See C. Liao et al., "Study on the Distribution and Quantity of Biomass Residues Resource in China," *Biomass and Bioenergy*, vol. 27 (2004), pp. 111–17, and Z. Yuan, "Research and Development on Biomass Energy in China," China Biomass Development Center, available at www.frankhaugwitz.info. One estimate of an upper bound on this resource is 175 million tons, per Larson et al., op. cit. note 10. However, CREIA (unpublished, 2007) estimates a much larger quantity of forest residues, 440–520 million tons, with further increases possible because of the government's tree planting programs.

12. See Larson et al., op. cit. note 10 for higher scenarios. One unpublished analysis by co-author Cathy Kunkel shows 80 gigawatts (GW) as an upper bound using the following assumptions. Assuming 370 million tons per year of crop residues, with heating value at 16 gigajoules (GJ) per ton, plus 150 million tons of forest residues, with heating value of 17 GJ/ton, yields 8.5 exajoule (EJ) total resource. Assuming plant capacity factor of 80 percent and average efficiency of 25 percent (typical for a 25 MW plant), total plant capacity for using the 8.5 EJ would be 84 GW.

13. See Wang Gehua et al., *Liquid Biofuels for Transportation: Chinese Potential and Implications for Sustainable Agriculture and Energy in the 21st Century* (Eschborn, Germany: GTZ, 2006); Gu Shuhua and Zen Ling, "The Development Potential of Biofuel in China," in *Proceedings of China Renewable Energy Development Strategy Workshop, Beijing, 28 October 2005*, op. cit. note 6; B. Yang and Y. Lu, "The Promise of Cellulosic Ethanol Production in China," *Journal of Chemical Technology and Biotechnology*, vol. 82 (2007), pp. 6–10; Worldwatch Institute, *Biofuels for Transport: Global Potential and Implications for Sustainable Agriculture and Energy in the 21st Century* (London: Earthscan, 2007).

14. The nine provinces are Anhui, Hebei, Helongjiang, Henan, Hubei, Jiangsu, Jilin, Liaoning, and Shangdong. Four of these provinces (Hebei, Hubei, Jiangsu, and Shandong) only had partial mandates for blending in major cities. Four major biofuels producers sell their output to the China National Petroleum Corporation, which then blends and sells the E10 fuel in the nine provinces.

15. Renewable Energy Policy Network for the 21st Century (REN21), *Renewables 2007 Global Status Report* (Paris: REN21 and Washington, DC: Worldwatch Institute, forthcoming).

16. "Food Price Rises Force a Cut in Biofuels," *Times Online*, 12 June 2007.

17. Wang et al., op. cit. note 13; NDRC, "China's Long and Middle-Term Renewable Energy Plan" (Beijing:

Endnotes

2007), announced and summarized by *Xinhua News Agency*, 4 September 2007.

18. Wang et al., op. cit. note 13. Original estimate is for 2.5 million tons of ethanol. Tons converted into liters using the conversion factor of 1,260 liters/ton (average density 0.79), per REN21, op cit. note 15.

19. Wang et al., op. cit. note 13; K. Latner, C. O'Kray, and J. Jiang, "China Bio-Fuels: An Alternative Future for Agriculture," GAIN Report No. CH6049 (Washington, DC: U.S. Department of Agriculture, Foreign Agriculture Service, 2006). Wang estimates ethanol from cassava in Guangxi and Guangdong, the main growing regions, at 0.77 million tons/year; Latner et al. estimate 4 million tons ethanol/year from cassava. Conversions per note 18.

20. Wang et al., op. cit. note 13. Estimate is for 1.38 million tons/year; conversion per note 18.

21. Worldwatch Institute, op. cit. note 13; Yang and Lu, op. cit. note 13.

22. REN21, op. cit. note 15.

23. Latner et al., op. cit. note 19.

24. Ibid.; J. Sheehan et al., "Energy and Environmental Aspects of Using Corn Stove for Fuel Ethanol," *Journal of Industrial Ecology*, vol. 7 (2003), pp. 117–46; Lang and Yu, op. cit. note 12. Ethanol estimate by co-author Cathy Kunkel (unpublished) as follows: Assuming average residue heating value of 16 GJ/ton, cellulose to ethanol conversion efficiency of 340 liters/dry ton of biomass (per Sheehan et al., op. cit. this note), and half of total residues available, or 4.25 EJ/year, and a heating value for ethanol of 26.7 GJ/ton, 70 million tons/year of ethanol, or 90 billion liters/year, could be produced. Yang and Lu, op. cit. note 13, estimates cellulosic ethanol potential at 640 billion liters, based on converting all available crop and forest residues, as well as establishing energy crop plantations on 10 percent of all farmland, pastures, and woodlands; but this seems to be an unrealistic scenario.

25. Cao Ting, "Hui Cong Industry Research Report," 9 August 2007, available at http://hc360.com. Figure of 70 billion is converted from 52 million tons using a conversion factor of 1,360 liters/ton for gasoline, per www.simetric.co.uk/si_liquids.htm.

26. Actual biodiesel production in 2006 was about 57 million liters. Wang et al., op. cit. note 13; W. Wen, "Biodiesel in China," presented at the Motor Vehicle Emission Control Workshop, Hong Kong, 10 May 2006, available at www.cse.polyu.edu.hk.

27. Wang et al., op. cit. note 13. Estimate is 3–4 million tons/year. Tons of biodiesel converted into liters using the conversion factor of 1,130 liters/ton (average density 0.88), from REN21, op. cit. note 15.

28. At least 2 million hectares (ha) are available for planting jatropha, with an average yield of 9.75 tons of kernel per ha; the biodiesel yield can be up to 3 tons per ha, implying that at least 3.25 tons of jatropha kernel are needed to make 1 ton biodiesel. See Wang et al., op. cit. note 13; Wen, op. cit. note 26. Given these assumptions, biodiesel potential is about 6 million tons. New jatropha plantations were in progress in Yunnan province, but there were concerns about environmental loss and whether "waste forestlands" designated for the plantations were really that. See Yingling Liu, "Chinese Biofuels Expansion Threatens Ecological Balance," Renewable Energy Access.com, 27 March 2007. Yunnan plans to become China's premier source of biofuels by 2015, achieving 4 million tons of ethanol and 0.6 million tons of biodiesel. Conversions per note 27.

29. In addition, the waste from producing ethanol from sweet sorghum can be used to produce biodiesel. The Chinese Academy of Agricultural Sciences is developing a hybrid rapeseed plant with very high oil content specifically for biodiesel.

30. Wang et al., op. cit, note 13; Latner et al., op. cit. note 19. Estimate is 19 million tons; conversion per note 27.

31. There are concerns about environmental impacts of palm oil plantations outside of China that export to Chinese biodiesel producers. See Jiao Li, "Biodiesel Sweeps China in Controversy," RenewableEnergyAccess.com, 23 January 2007.

32. CREIA, unpublished estimates, 2007. Estimates are 50 million tons total, 28 million tons ethanol, and 24 million tons biodiesel. Conversions per note 27.

33. Zhao Yongqiang and Wang Zhongying, China Energy Research Institute, unpublished estimates (Beijing: 2007). Estimates are 15 million tons by 2020 and 35 million tons by 2030. Conversions per note 27.

34. See Table 2. Targets are for 10 million tons ethanol and 2 million tons biodiesel; conversions per notes 18 and 27. Globally, the International Energy Agency projects up to 120 billion liters of ethanol by 2020, up from 37 billion liters per year in 2006, if biofuels policies continue to proliferate and accelerate, per Lew Fulton, *Biofuels for Transport* (Paris: International Energy Agency, 2003). The government's ethanol target by 2020, if fulfilled, would probably allow the governments planned E10 (10%) blending of ethanol with all gasoline nationwide by 2020.

35. Liu, op. cit. note 28.

36. Worldwatch Institute, op. cit. note 13.

37. International Energy Agency, *Energy Technology Perspectives: Scenarios and Strategies to 2050* (Paris: 2006).

38. Li Zheng et al., "Polygeneration Energy System Based on Coal Gasification," *Energy for Sustainable Development*, vol. 7, no. 4 (2003), pp. 57–62.

39. Jack Perkowski, "The Battle for China's Auto Market," presented at JPMorgan's "Hands-On China Series," Beijing, April 2007 (Hong Kong: JPMorgan, 2007).

40. "State Grid Develops Electric Cars," *China Daily*, 27 April 2007; "Carmakers to Roll Out Hybrid Vehicles," *China Daily*, 27 April 2007.

China's Renewable Energy Future

1. National Development and Reform Commission (NDRC), "Medium and Long-Term Development Plan for Renewable Energy in China" (Beijing: September 2007); Emma Graham-Harrison, "China Plans $265

Endnotes

Billion Renewables Spending," *Reuters*, 4 September 2007.

2. Li Junfeng, *Wind-12* (Beijing: Chemical Press, 2005).

3. U.S. prices given include subsidies such as the national Production Tax Credit, which was 1.9 cents per kilowatt-hour in 2007. European prices are feed-in prices set by governments, with the highest costs shared among the electric utility customer base. For more on these policies and prices, see REN21, Renewable Energy Policy Network for the 21st Century (REN21), *Renewables 2007 Global Status Report* (Paris: REN21 and Washington, DC: Worldwatch Institute, forthcoming).

4. Sidebar 7 from the following sources: Ma Xuelu, Director, Administrative Committee, Baoding New High-Tech Industrial Development Zone, personal communication, 10 May 2007; Ma Xuelu, presentation at groundbreaking ceremony of wind power industrial park in China's Electricity Valley, 13 March 2007; "Baoding Constructs Hub for New Energy Industry," *China Environment Online*, 11 August 2003; Wang Yijuan, "China's First Energy Equipment Industrial Base Showed Potential," *Economic Reference News*, 31 August 2005; "Baoding High-tech Park Leading Domestic New Energy Equipment Industry," *China News Service Hebei Branch*, 5 December 2005.

5. See Eric Martinot, "World Bank Energy Projects in China: Influences on Environmental Protection," *Energy Policy*, vol. 29, no. 8 (2001), pp. 581–94, and various project and organizational web sites, including www.cresp.org.cn, www2.gtz.de/china/chinese/english/environmentlist.htm, www.energyandenvironment.org, www.ccre.com.cn, and www.efchina.org/programs.renew.cfm.

6. Sidebar 8 from the following sources: China Energy Research Institute (ERI) and Lawrence Berkeley Lab (LBL), "China's Sustainable Energy Future: Scenarios of Energy and Carbon Emissions" (Berkeley, CA: LBL, and Beijing: ERI, 2003). Note that 40 gigawatts (GW) of small hydro was achieved in 2005, just a few years after the ERI/LBL study, and 15 years ahead of their scenario. Other aspects of the 2002 scenario have also been quickly eclipsed by events, including total energy consumption; Ni Weidou and Thomas Johansson, "Energy for Sustainable Development in China," *Energy Policy*, vol. 32, no. 10 (2004), pp. 1225–29; China Task Force on Energy Strategies and Technologies, "Transforming Coal for Sustainability: A Strategy for China," Report to the China Council for International Cooperation on Environment and Development, *Energy for Sustainable Development*, vol. 7, no. 4 (2003), pp. 5–14; World Business Council on Sustainable Development, "Pathways to 2050: Energy and Climate Change," (Geneva: 2005); Zhang Xiliang and He Jiankun, "Strategies and Policies on Promoting Massive Renewable Energy Development," in *Proceedings of China Renewable Energy Development Strategy Workshop, Beijing, 28 October 2005* (Beijing: Tsinghua University Institute of Nuclear and New Energy Technology and Tsinghua-BP Clean Energy Research and Education Center, 2005).

7. Eric Martinot et al., "Renewable Energy Futures: Targets, Scenarios, and Pathways," *Annual Review of Environment and Resources*, vol. 32 (2007), forthcoming.

8. Based on national development targets; see Table 2.

9. Estimated from Chinese Renewable Energy Industries Association (CREIA).

10. CREIA estimates 100 GW of wind by 2030 and 500–600 GW by 2040–2050. An "advanced" scenario shows China with 330 GW by 2030, per Global Wind Energy Council and Greenpeace, "Global Wind Energy Outlook 2006" (Brussels: 2006). The 600 GW of wind power by 2050 would generate 1,500 terrawatt-hours (TWh), or the equivalent of 300 GW of coal power.

11. KPMG Huazhen, "Alternative Energies in China: Which Way Will the Wind Blow?" (Beijing: 2007), p. 7. This would generate 1,200 TWh by 2050, or the equivalent of 250 GW of coal-fired power.

12. REN21, op. cit. note 3; Martinot et al., op. cit. note 7.

13. In contrast to solar PV, solar thermal power may remain practical only on large multi-megawatt scales. Solar thermal power employs the sun's heat to create steam and run a conventional steam-cycle power generator. This is in marked contrast to solar PV, which converts sunlight directly in electricity and can be placed on virtually any rooftop or exposed surface. China's "Medium- and Long-Term Renewable Energy Development Plan" (NDRC, op. cit. note 1) includes a target for 200 megawatts of solar thermal power.

14. National development target (see Table 2) and CREIA estimates. This would generate about 1,050–1,250 TWh, or the equivalent of 260–300 GW of coal power generation.

15. There is growing interest in using geothermal heat pumps in China for supplying heating and hot water at the building level, and some believe it could make an important contribution. See National Renewable Energy Laboratory, "Development of the Geothermal Heat Pump Market in China" (Golden, CO: 2006).

Index

A

Acciona wind manufacturer, 19
acid rain, 10
agriculture, 28–31, 43n10
air pollution, 6, 8–12, 31
Asian Development Bank, 33
Asia-Pacific Partnership, 33
Australia, 24
automobiles, sales of, 10

B

Baoding New High-Tech Industrial Development
    Zone, 33
Baoding Tianwei-Yingli, 23
Beijing
    air pollution in, 10, 31
    natural gas buses in, 31
    renewable energy strategy, 33
    solar power in, 21
Benxi City, 8
biofuels
    investments in, 7
    policies for, 29
    renewable energy goals, 14
    sources of, 29–31
    subsidies for, 29
    technology prognosis for, 31, 36
biogas
    investments in, 7
    household use of, 29
    power generation from, 28
    renewable energy goals, 14
    taxes on, 15
    technology prognosis for, 36
biomass gasification, 42n2
biomass pellets, 29
biomass power
    plant limitations, 29
    renewable energy capacity, 16, 28
    renewable energy goals, 14–15, 42n2
    sources of, 6–7, 28–29
    technology prognosis for, 34–35
BIPV (building-integrated photovoltaics), 21–22, 35
Brightness Program, 22

C

carbon emissions, 10–11, 34, 38n31
CDM (Clean Development Mechanism), 18, 33
cellulosic ethanol, 7, 30–31, 36
Chen Deming, 32
China Energy Research Institute, 31, 34
China National Petroleum Corporation, 43n14
China Power Investment, 20
China Renewable Energy Scale-Up Program (CRESP), 33
China Sunergy, 22–23
Chinese Meteorological Research Institute, 17–18, 33
Chinese Renewable Energy Industries Association
    (CREIA), 30–31
Chinese Task Force on Energy Strategies and
    Technologies, 34
clean coal technology, 6
Clean Development Mechanism (CDM), 18, 33
coal
    biomass power and, 31
    clean coal technology, 6
    consumption of, 9–10
    converting to liquid fuels, 31
    energy-intensity improvements, 34
concession policy for wind power, 15, 17–18, 33

D

Dabancheng Wind Farm, 35
Datang power-generating company, 19
Denmark, 19
Dezhou City, 27
Dong Fang Steam Turbine Works, 19

E

economic development, 10–12
electric vehicles, 31
electricity
    capacity, 9, 13, 34
    consumption of, 9–10
    direct energy value of, 39n4
    energy efficiency and, 11
    from renewable sources, 13, 34
    rural programs, 22
    technology prognosis for, 35
energy consumption, 9–13
energy efficiency goals, 11

Index

Index

Other Worldwatch Reports

Worldwatch Reports provide in-depth, quantitative, and qualitative analysis of the major issues affecting prospects for a sustainable society. The Reports are written by members of the Worldwatch Institute research staff or outside specialists and are reviewed by experts unaffiliated with Worldwatch. They are used as concise and authoritative references by governments, non-governmental organizations, businesses, and educational institutions worldwide.

On Climate Change, Energy, and Materials

169: Mainstreaming Renewable Energy in the 21st Century, 2004
160: Reading the Weathervane: Climate Policy From Rio to Johannesburg, 2002
157: Hydrogen Futures: Toward a Sustainable Energy System, 2001
151: Micropower: The Next Electrical Era, 2000
149: Paper Cuts: Recovering the Paper Landscape, 1999
144: Mind Over Matter: Recasting the Role of Materials in Our Lives, 1998
138: Rising Sun, Gathering Winds: Policies To Stabilize the Climate and Strengthen Economies, 1997

On Ecological and Human Health

174: Oceans in Peril: Protecting Marine Biodiversity, 2007
165: Winged Messengers: The Decline of Birds, 2003
153: Why Poison Ourselves: A Precautionary Approach to Synthetic Chemicals, 2000
148: Nature's Cornucopia: Our Stakes in Plant Diversity, 1999
145: Safeguarding the Health of Oceans, 1999
142: Rocking the Boat: Conserving Fisheries and Protecting Jobs, 1998
141: Losing Strands in the Web of Life: Vertebrate Declines and the Conservation of Biological Diversity, 1998
140: Taking a Stand: Cultivating a New Relationship With the World's Forests, 1998

On Economics, Institutions, and Security

173: Beyond Disasters: Creating Opportunities for Peace, 2007
168: Venture Capitalism for a Tropical Forest: Cocoa in the Mata Atlântica, 2003
167: Sustainable Development for the Second World: Ukraine and the Nations in Transition, 2003
166: Purchasing Power: Harnessing Institutional Procurement for People and the Planet, 2003
164: Invoking the Spirit: Religion and Spirituality in the Quest for a Sustainable World, 2002
162: The Anatomy of Resource Wars, 2002
159: Traveling Light: New Paths for International Tourism, 2001
158: Unnatural Disasters, 2001

On Food, Water, Population, and Urbanization

172: Catch of the Day: Choosing Seafood for Healthier Oceans
171: Happer Meals: Rethinking the Global Meat Industry, 2005
170: Liquid Assets: The Critical Need to Safeguard Freshwater Ecosytems, 2005
163: Home Grown: The Case for Local Food in a Global Market, 2002
161: Correcting Gender Myopia: Gender Equity, Women's Welfare, and the Environment, 2002
156: City Limits: Putting the Brakes on Sprawl, 2001
154: Deep Trouble: The Hidden Threat of Groundwater Pollution, 2000
150: Underfed and Overfed: The Global Epidemic of Malnutrition, 2000
147: Reinventing Cities for People and the Planet, 1999

To see our complete list of Reports, visit www.worldwatch.org/taxonomy/term/40

The Worldwatch Institute is an independent research organization that works for an environmentally sustainable and socially just society, in which the needs of all people are met without threatening the health of the natural environment or the well-being of future generations. By providing compelling, accessible, and fact-based analysis of critical global issues, Worldwatch informs people around the world about the complex interactions among people, nature, and economies. Worldwatch focuses on the underlying causes of and practical solutions to the world's problems, in order to inspire people to demand new policies, investment patterns, and lifestyle choices.

Support for the Institute is provided by the Blue Moon Fund, the German Government, the Richard and Rhoda Goldman Fund, The Goldman Environmental Prize, the W. K. Kellogg Foundation, the Marianists of the USA, the Norwegian Royal Ministry of Foreign Affairs, the V. Kann Rasmussen Foundation, The Shared Earth Foundation, The Shenandoah Foundation, the Sierra Club, the United Nations Population Fund, the United Nations Environment Programme, the Wallace Genetic Foundation, Inc., the Wallace Global Fund, the Johanette Wallerstein Institute, and the Winslow Foundation. The Institute also receives financial support from many individual donors who share our commitment to a more sustainable society.

Published August 2007 | $95.00
ISBN: 978-1-84407-422-8

This landmark report includes:
- Status and Global Trends
- New Technologies, Crops and Prospects
- Key Economic and Social Issues
- Key Environmental Issues
- Market Introduction and Technology Strategies
- Policy Framework
- Recommendations for Decision-Makers

biofuels
FOR TRANSPORT

"A compelling synthesis of the current and future trends in biofuels, with a thorough assessment of actions that must be taken to ensure the sustainable development of this industry."
—*Amory B. Lovins, Chairman and Chief Scientist, RMI*

"An essential treatment of this vital subject."
—*Vinod Khosla, Khosla Ventures, USA*

"...a tour de force through the complex array of issues associated with rapidly expanding biofuels markets around the world."
—*Julia Marton-Lefevre, Director General, IUCN*

Biofuels for Transport is a unique and comprehensive assessment of the opportunities and risks of the large-scale production of biofuels, which demystifies complex questions and concerns, such as the "food v. fuel" debate. Global in scope, it includes five country studies from Brazil, China, Germany, India, and Tanzania. The authors conclude that biofuels will play a significant role in our energy future, but warn that the large-scale use of biofuels carries risks that require focused and immediate policy initiatives.

Four Easy Ways to Order!
- Call: 1-877-539-9946
- Fax: 1-301-567-9553
- E-mail: wwpub@worldwatch.org
- Complete and mail this form to:
  Worldwatch Institute
  PO Box 879
  Oxon Hill, MD 20750-9909

WORLDWATCH INSTITUTE
www.worldwatch.org

Yes, please send me a copy of *Biofuels for Transport* today!
(Minimum shipping US: $9, Canada: $36, International: $41)

Method of payment: ☐ Check enclosed *(payable to Worldwatch in U.S. Dollars only)*
☐ VISA   ☐ Mastercard   ☐ AMEX   ☐ Discover

Credit Card No.   Exp. Date

Signature

Name (please print)

Address

City/State/Country   Zip/Postal Code

Phone   E-mail address   Promo Code: CHSR

THE WORLDWATCH INSTITUTE

VITAL SIGNS 2007-2008

The Trends That Are Shaping Our Future

VITAL SIGNS 2007-2008

▶▶ **23 new trends in this edition!**

▶▶ **Total of 44 trends covering 6 categories**

▶▶ **Analysis of each trend gives context and interconnections, plus, charts and graphs provide visual comparisons of each trend over time**

CATEGORIES OF TRENDS

▶▶ Food and Agriculture

▶▶ Energy and Environment

▶▶ Social and Economic

▶▶ Transportation and Communications

▶▶ Conflict and Peace

▶▶ Health

VITAL SIGNS 2007-2008

— **$18.95 plus S&H** —

Five Easy Ways To Order:

▶▶ Call: 1-877-539-9946

▶▶ Fax: 1-301-567-9553

▶▶ E-mail: wwpub@worldwatch.org

▶▶ Online: www.worldwatch.org

▶▶ Mail your order to: Worldwatch Institute, PO Box 879, Oxon Hill, MD 20750-0879

Promo Code: CHSR

"The most straightforward and reliable environmental, economic, and social information available on the entire planet Earth."
—Michael Pastore, ePublishers Weekly

"It's cool appraisal of our planet makes all other works of reference look trivial."
—The Guardian

"A key source of hard facts on global trends."
—Booklist

WWW.WORLDWATCH.ORG